PRAISE FOR *INSPIRING EXCELLENCE*

Michael Schutzler takes you through a journey of experience and a broad range of leadership dimensions. *Inspiring Excellence* is both comprehensive and insightful. I highly recommend the book for leaders who want to up their game.

Jim Wiggett, CEO
Jackson Hole Group

Inspiring Excellence is a lightning strike of clarity and simplicity. Michael Schutzler distills the profound principles of great leadership into basic and clear precepts of action and relationship. His model draws from what we all experience and know but can't seem to pin down. He does!

Sandy Gould, VP Human Resources
Linden Lab – creators of *SecondLife*

This well-organized, thoughtful book distills a broad topic down to very specific, actionable, and practical tools for sharpening leadership skills. I intend to keep a copy in the top drawer of my desk for handy reference and as a periodic reminder of the blueprint for effective leadership.

Paul Goodrich, Managing Director
Madrona Venture Group

Michael Schutzler has done a great job explaining leadership skills and practice in a way that applies to any situation, including the way a person leads his or her life. *Inspiring Excellence* is filled with great examples of applying real leadership skills in real situations.

Aaron Finn, CEO
AdReady.com

Michael Schutzler took his many years of real world experience and learning and translated it into a compelling must-read. I am recommending this book to everyone in my professional network.

Brett Thompson, SVP Human Resources
Classmates Online

Inspiring Excellence presents an approach to leadership that works even in the "double bottom line" setting of a non-profit organization.

Tom Donlea, Executive Director
Merchant Risk Council

INSPIRING EXCELLENCE

A PATH TO EXCEPTIONAL LEADERSHIP

MICHAEL SCHUTZLER

BOOK PUBLISHERS NETWORK

Book Publishers Network
P.O. Box 2256
Bothell • WA • 98041
PH • 425-483-3040
www.bookpublishersnetwork.com

Graphic clipart © 2009 Jupiterimages Corporation

10 9 8 7 6 5 4 3 2 1

Printed in the United States of America

LCCN 2009924891
ISBN10 1-935359-10-X
ISBN13 978-1-935359-10-4

The excerpt from Dr. Martin Luther King Jr.'s "I have a dream" speech in Chapter 5 is reprinted by arrangement with The Heirs to the Estate of Martin Luther King Jr., c/o Writers House as agent for the proprietor New York, NY. © 1963 Dr. Martin Luther King Jr.; Copyright renewed 1991 Coretta Scott King.

Anecdotes Disclaimer
The characters and situations in this book are from actual experience. The names of most individuals and organizations have been changed, and some details have been adjusted to make it harder to pinpoint who, what, where, and when. This has been done to protect individuals from unwanted attention while preserving the lessons that their actions provide for all of us.

Results Disclaimer
To the fullest extent permitted by applicable law, Book Publishers Network and Michael Schutzler each make no representations or warranties of any kind, express or implied, regarding the use of or results of the recommended exercises or the results of the opinions presented in this book.

Editor: Julie Scandora
Cover Designer: Laura Zugzda
Typographer: Stephanie Martindale

For Megan and Erik

Contents

Foreword xi

Acknowledgements. xiii

Introduction

Chapter 1: Why Leadership Matters 3

    One Selfless Act 5

Chapter 2: Leadership is Learned. 9

    A Scrappy Start. 10

Chapter 3: A Leadership Curriculum 15

Part I: Fundamental Leadership Skills

Chapter 4: Listening 23

    Pay Attention. 24

    Are You Listening?. 25

    Listen and Learn. 27

    Listening Inspires 29

Chapter 5: Storytelling. 31

    Cultivate Confidence 32

    Be Authentic 34

    Push Yourself. 35

    Spontaneous Storytelling 36

    Exercising Eloquence 37

    Treasure Hunting 38

    Stories Move Mountains 39

Chapter 6: Negotiating. 43

    The Negotiation Cycle. 45

Making the Request 46
Making the Commitment. 48
A Variation on Commitment. 49
Declaring the Obstacle 50
Lead by Example. 52

Chapter 7: Assessing People 55
Setting Standards 57
Make Them Your Own 60
Making Private Assessments 61
Stand Back and Assess. 62
Sharing Assessments. 63
Deliver Powerful Praise 64
Building Goodwill. 64
Tell Them You Noticed 66
Make Effective Criticisms. 67
Counterproductive Criticism. 68
Making a Sandwich 69
Be Demanding *and* Constructive 70

Part II: Essential Leadership Functions

Chapter 8: Assembling Talent. 75
Relationships Are the Source. 76
Attracting Talent. 77
Choosing the Right Talent 79
Discipline Defeats Talent 80
Diversity Is the Key 81
Multidisciplinary Crisis. 82
Sad but True .84
Bucking the Stereotype 85
Deliberate Transformation 86
Merging Talent. 87

Chapter 9: Reaching Consensus. 91
    The Moses Model 92
    The Trump Model 94
    Gladiator versus Emperor. 95
    The Socrates Model 96
    Fostering Respectful Debate 97
    Converting Assertions into Questions. 99
    Cutting to the Chase. 101
    Consensus Becomes Conviction 102

Chapter 10: Making Tough Choices 105
    Cultivate Courage 106
    Shouting into the Chasm 109
    Facing Your Fear. 110
    Checklist for Choosing 112
    Choosing Everything Is Choosing Nothing. . . . 113
    Choice Creates Possibilities. 114
    Start Simple. 116
    Alea Iacta Est. 118

Chapter 11: Harnessing Ambition 123
    It's Not about You 124
    Corporate Chiefs. 126
    Reverend Shepherds. 126
    Nation Builders 127
    Hope Is Your Engine. 128
    Get On with It 130

Appendix A: Hiring a Coach 135
    When to Hire a Coach. 136
    How Does Coaching Work? 137
    How Do You Pick a Coach?. 138

Appendix B: Sample Assessment Rubric. 139

Notes & Sources 143
About the Author. 157

Foreword

Peter Drucker, the late prolific author and prophetic econo-mist[1] once said, "Management is doing things right. Leadership is doing the right things." This concise definition makes it possible to declare that this is not a book about management. This is a book about leadership. There are many wonderful books, essays, blogs, and seminars on "doing things right," which describe best practices for supervising employees, time management, change management, process improvement, and much more. This book does not address those topics, at least not directly. Instead, this book describes an approach to "doing the right things" that will inspire and motivate the people you are leading.

Few men or women have both the ambition and courage required to step up and lead. You must be among those few; why else would you be reading this? If you are already in a leadership role or aspire to lead, I hope this book is useful to you. I have spent more than two decades studying and practi leadership in a wide assortment of industries, countries, and organizations. In the process, I have read many books and essays and have learned from some brilliant and some not-so-brilliant executives, entrepreneurs, military commanders, and government officials. I have also had the opportunity to succeed and fail as I've tried my own hand at leadership. This book is filled with perspectives, examples, and suggestions distilled from my observations, experimentation, and quite a bit of thrashing around.

At the suggestion of those who helped steer this project, the very wide topic of leadership has been compressed into a brief text focused more on the practical than the theoretical. If you at least conditionally accept the assertions and apply the exercises recommended in this book, you will open yourself to shedding habits and assumptions that cloud your judgment. You will then be free to function from a perspective of clear intention as you employ both your intellect and insight. That shift in behavior will allow your finest attributes and strength of character consistently to inform your observations, your decisions, and your actions. Following Mr. Drucker's encouragement then comes easily. You will naturally do the right thing in the midst of striving to do it right.

Thank you for investing the effort to read this book. I sincerely hope it gives you much more in return.

Michael Schutzler
Seattle
January 2009

ACKNOWLEDGEMENTS

First and foremost, I would like to thank my tireless editor Erin Pursell, who was always collaborative and insightful and without whom this book could not have been completed. Thanks also to those who helped review the early, messy stages of the manuscript and who generously gave encouragement and expertise, especially Father Patrick Clark, Jon Ingalls, Tim Lerch JDPSN, Karim Meghji, Margaret Moore, Stephen Schramke, and Beth Whitman. I am indebted to the publishing team of Sheryn Hara, Stephanie Martindale, Julie Scandora, and Laura Zugzda, whose workmanship and talent created an elegant finished product. Finally, my deepest gratitude goes to Cari—my companion, love, and wife of fifteen years, who patiently endured many months of my obsessive distraction while I worked on this project.

Introduction

Why Leadership Matters

Leadership is Learned

A Leadership Curriculum

CHAPTER 1

WHY LEADERSHIP MATTERS

When we try to pick anything out by itself,
we find it hitched to everything else in the universe.

John Muir[2]

L eadership is a relationship. It is a relationship in which one person inspires and motivates a group to make sustained effort toward a common goal. Although your achievements are a measure of your competence, those achievements are not yours. They are the outcome of your relationships with your staff, chain of command, partners, customers, and community. Even the most superb results that come directly from your decisions do not matter nearly as much as how you make those decisions. It is your behavior over the course of time that motivates and inspires those whom you lead. Leadership is neither a solo performance nor a one-time event. It is an intricate web of relationships linking people with a common hope. Build this web and you succeed; break it and you fail.

The actions and decisions of every leader have significant impact. This is obvious if you lead a worldwide organization of thirty thousand people but is just as true if you lead a team of only three people. Your actions and decisions affect the live of your team, their families, their friends, your organization's partners and stakeholders, your own life, and therefore your own family and friends. You don't have to be president, prime minister, or chief executive officer to make a big impact.

Furthermore, your influence is even more widespread than the people you lead today. How you lead today creates ripples that multiply your impact over time. Your ambitions, decisions, and actions become the stories of successes and failures. Those stories—the hopes, the wins and losses, the painfully boring parts, the stunning surprises, and everything in between— will be told for years by the people you have affected directly and indirectly. Failed Internet start-ups from the last decade released employees who now work for new technology companies. These hardened employees laugh and weep about the lessons learned in those heady days. It has been the same in public education for decades—as one school district succeeds or fails, it becomes the benchmark and inspiration for another.

Every field of endeavor is like this. The stories of your attempts to lead for better or worse will be used as role models or cautionary tales and will motivate someone to pursue a leadership role, which restarts the cycle of ambition, decision, action, and impact. The influence of one human being who takes on even a small leadership role is felt in thousands of lives for years to come. This point brings to mind a merchant family I once worked with in Jordan many years ago.

> Leadership is a relationship in which one person inspires and motivates a group to make sustained effort toward a common goal.

ONE SELFLESS ACT

Amir was a young father and husband, born and raised in the city of Nablus. In the hot summer of 1967, he and his young family, along with thousands of other Palestinians, fled the Arab-Israeli war that raged for six days.[3] He left his home, his business, and his wealth behind to join many others in Jordan to wait out the conflict and hope for an end so they could return home. When it was finally safe to return, Amir learned Nablus had been occupied, his home had been destroyed, and Israeli settlers—defended by their military—had laid claim to his land. Rather than become a bitter man like many of his peers, he decided to start a new life in the city of Amman, Jordan. He became a merchant and distributor at a small shop of his own, where he bought and sold paper products. He was a clever man, a hard-working man, and above all, a man of his word.

Amir conducted himself with honor for many years, hired well, made a decent profit, and made many strong business friendships in his adopted country. His sons Munir and Tarek worked as his assistants. They were bright and enthusiastic and in time joined Amir at business meetings held in the traditional manner over long lunches—they sampled Mediterranean dishes, drank sweet aromatic coffee, had conversations about life and family, and afterward conducted business negotiations while sharing a water pipe with rich tobacco.

At one lunch, Amir was presented with an opportunity to make a very large profit because his supplier had made several errors in calculating requirements for a certain paper. Amir calmly pointed out the errors to the surprised and grateful supplier. Tarek and Munir both were stunned at Amir's willingness to give up an enormous profit and confronted him afterward. Amir sat in silence for a moment and sighed before explaining, "If I had kept silent, I would only have money. What you gain today at the expense of others will cost you much more tomorrow. I'd rather have that man's trust for the next twenty years."

Tarek and Munir studied everything about their father's approach to business. After their long apprenticeship, Amir asked his sons to begin running the business. They did so eagerly and applied their own passions into lines of business that Amir never imagined entering. They added engineering services, farming equipment, telecommunications systems, and transportation. The little paper business expanded. They hired hundreds of employees, established partnerships with companies throughout Europe and the United States, and worked with large commercial enterprises and government agencies to modernize the Jordanian infrastructure.

One man, who could have easily justified a bitter worldview after losing his home, understood that conduct is more important than immediate profit, even an immense profit, and inspired two others to operate under such high principles as well. In time, they built a venture that benefited millions of people across a nation.

As Amir's family story teaches, leadership matters in every facet of life. Although it is clear that more than a few heads of state could use some help, this book was not written with them in mind. This book is for every entrepreneur, executive, abbot, department head, project manager, little league coach, firehouse chief, pastor, lieutenant, parent-teacher association chair, and anyone else who has the occasion to inspire and motivate others. When you have the rare opportunity to lead, make the most of it. Be ambitious and aspire to be a great leader because you can and, yes, it matters. Every person who leads has a significant influence on many lives, long after their moment has passed. Every leader has the opportunity to build relationships that create a better world. If you already agree or at least are willing to consider sincerely the premise that leadership is relationship, then you are already on the path to exceptional leadership.

CHAPTER 2

LEADERSHIP IS LEARNED

Give me a fruitful error any time,
full of seeds, bursting with its own corrections.
You can keep your sterile truth for yourself.

Vilfredo Pareto[4]

For most of human history, prevailing wisdom has dictated that leaders are born. Society has also commonly accepted that leaders are born only in certain families. Anyone outside this stock who shows aptitude for leadership is generally considered an ill-equipped upstart or opportunist. History is replete with examples. Consider the famous King Henry IV of England, aptly portrayed by Shakespeare as an embattled monarch defending his claim to the throne against cousins, friends, and enemies who argued he wasn't a rightful heir.[5] Or consider the less well known but equally intriguing Habibullah Ghazi of Afghanistan, a Tajik despised by rival Pashtuns as a mere "son of a water carrier" unworthy of leading their people.[6] These are just two of the countless usurpers from every culture, country and period of history. The belief in proper parentage as a requisite for leadership, however, is not just an artifact from history or confined to royal bloodlines. It continues today in walks of life.

A Scrappy Start

My father is a naturalized American citizen who was born in 1936 in what is now Lithuania. He fled the Russian army as a child and later successfully escaped from East to West Berlin as a young man with only the clothes on his back. He was able to find work in the German government as a cartographer but was not able to attend a German university because he was a poor refugee from the wrong side of the wall. He worked hard and eventually decided that the limits to his career and economic aspirations were too much to bear. In 1960 he made the fateful decision to leave his homeland and, with the flip of a coin, chose a job in Chicago over a job in Johannesburg.

This optimistic, spirited German immigrated with his young wife to the United States and once again started over, poor but determined. He worked three jobs for nearly a decade until he finally achieved a promotion that allowed him to focus on one job. In the following twenty years, my father consistently built strong relationships with peers, managers, and industry leaders in the field of cartography by always delivering on his commitments. He was a highly respected professional who found it easy to attract the best and brightest talent in his line of work. By the early 1980s, he was a leader in his company and, with the help of his highly skilled and motivated staff, was an early adopter of Apple computer technology applied to map creation and display. His company pursued this new course of digitized mapping and evolved to become MapQuest, the online mapping service, which subsequently inspired even more innovations that we now take for granted, such as Google Earth, the remarkable geographic visualization system used by almost every news broadcaster, and GPS-based navigation systems installed in millions of cars.

My father, now long retired, is the quintessential self-made man still respected in his field by former employees and industry peers. He was scrappy and tenacious, and undeniably an influential business leader, but he was hardly a member of the socioeconomic elite destined for greatness. Sadly, the notion of inherited leadership traits is not a relic of the past. It thrives and is still prevalent today in many highly educated, progressive organizations and cultures around the world. It is sad to me because it persists despite obviously flawed logic. If true leaders are only born in certain families, why wouldn't the successful leaders in every nation and every company and every university and every religious institution all be cousins? You have to admit that it's more than a bit of a stretch to think that on a planet with nearly six billion people, the millions of successful men and women running every company, university, government agency, military unit, nonprofit establishment, non-government organization, and religious institution all posess a shared gene with the Bill Gates clan. Or perhaps it's the Sir Winston Churchill family? Or is it the Mahatma Gandhi lineage? Wait, wait, I have it. Every leader is related to Nelson Mandela!

While the eugenics argument is quite silly, its corollary—the elite education argument—is just as outlandish. It is astounding to me how many times a person with an ivy-league education has been hired or promoted into a leadership role despite having clearly demonstrated a complete lack of skill, talent, or work ethic. So why does the prestigious ivy-league entry in candidate's curriculum vitae easily override good judgment logic on the part of many hiring managers? Unfortunately, an argument's lack of logic does not guarantee a lack of potency. The education pedigree works just as well as any prejudice or bias. Harvard and Oxford, for example, have very high standards for entry and have produced some fine leaders. However, this does not imply that a degree from Harvard or Oxford guarantees good leadership skills. Indeed, there are plenty of graduates from famous and highly respected universities who are best kept far way from leadership responsibilities.

Having poked a bit of fun at the genetic and education pedigree theories on leadership, it is time for an acknowledgment. All great leaders do have some points in common. Great leaders possess ambition—drive and determination to create something or achieve something widely believed impossible. Great leaders also recognize that leadership is a relationship and they have developed some very useful behaviors to make the most of that relationship. Fortunately for you and me, those behaviors can be learned and mastered by anyone with a will to do so.

Leadership is a set of learned behaviors, just as playing piano or riding a bicycle are learned behaviors. These activities are difficult at first and require a willingness to repeatedly fail and try again in order to master. Improvement only comes from error. You must be willing to hone your skills diligently with hard work and focus, regardless of family blood, race, color, religious tradition, social standing, educational background, other advantages you may think you have. The fundamental

> You must be willing to hone leadership diligently with hard work and focus, regardless of what advantages you may think you have.

skills and essential functions of leadership form the core of this book. You can master each of them. I am certain you agree at least in principle. If you didn't believe that leadership is learnable, you wouldn't be reading a book on leadership, now would you?

It is true that in every generation only a rare leader rises to the prominence of Lincoln, Gandhi, Gorbachev, or Mandela. Please understand, however, that their distinction arises because in one peculiar moment of history, those human beings were tested in ways that most observers find daunting, and their bold choices and selfless actions under duress continue to inspire

> Every act of leadership has the potential to make a significant impact.

long after the events are over. It is also true that every day an ordinary leader we never hear about makes bold choices and acts selflessly—a high school principal chooses how to handle a bomb threat, a fire chief chooses who to send into a burning building, or a coast guard lieutenant chooses how to set course during a storm to accomplish a rescue mission without losing the ship or crew at sea. Leadership greatness is tested in every moment of every day, all around the world. Every act of leadership has the potential to make a significant impact. You can be a great leader—regardless of the scope of your role.

After twenty-five years of studying and practicing leadership, it has become very clear to me that the tools you need to lead well are eyes, ears, nose, tongue, body, and mind. Leadership is a human endeavor. It is a relationship in which you inspire others to make a sustained effort toward a common goal. This means that how you interact with your team, your partners, and your sponsors is more important than your expertise or even yo results. The best indicator of your potential as a leader is the quality of the relationships you have with the people you influence.

If you remember nothing else from reading this book, please remember this: You already have all the tools you need to lead well. All that remains is determination and deliberate practice.

CHAPTER 3

A LEADERSHIP CURRICULUM

Learning without thought is labor lost.

Confucius[7]

Leadership is mastered the same way anything is mastered, a pound of practice for every ounce of theory. If you are lucky, you encounter a good teacher or mentor to help guide your skill development. Having a mentor is beneficial but only saves you the trouble of hunting and pecking for what to practice and when. In the end, it still comes down to practice. Your practice.

Why so much emphasis on practice? Since leadership is a relationship, every situation in which you engage other people is an essential part of your curriculum in the school of leadership. If you start now, every situation you encounter becomes an opportunity to develop your leadership skills, and if someday you acquire the title of president, director, general, or chief executive, you will be well prepared from all the practice you have exercised in your curriculum. And if you are already privileged enough to hold one of those titles, you owe it to yourself and your organization to perfect your leadership skills without delay.

Since practice makes perfect, the time to start leadership practice is now. To break leadership practice down into manageable components, we will use a straightforward learning framework. Effective leadership is composed of eight key elements, divided into two parts:

Part I
Fundamental Skills
Listening
Storytelling
Negotiating
Assessing

Part II
Essential Functions
Assembling Talent
Reaching Consensus
Making Tough Choices
Harnessing Ambition

Each of the eight elements in this learning framework will be explained in detail, along with practice recommendations. Anecdotes that help illustrate some of the points discussed in the text are offset in a shaded text box. Finally, each chapter ends with a short collection of "Quick Cues" that highlight essential concepts and serve as a prompt for future reference.

You already apply some of these leadership elements in your everyday relationships with family, friends, and colleagues. For example, if you have a reasonably successful marriage, it's likely that you

> The best indicator of your potential as a leader is the quality of the relationships you have with the people you influence.

first listen to your spouse and only then discuss conflicting options to reach agreement. In the same way, you must first listen to the people you wish to lead—to understand their perspective, insights, and potential contributions—before you can begin to negotiate and ultimately reach an agreement. Applying these elements to leadership requires specific intention. It is not enough to be a good spouse or parent. If you do not deliberately practice these elements and consciously choose to sharpen your leadership proficiency, then you will not have them to draw upon when the demands of leadership weigh heaviest.

When combined, these eight elements form a structure like a house.

In our house, the four skills of listening, storytelling, negotiating, and assessing serve as the foundation. When these four skills are well practiced, they create a firm, strong base for making tough choices, assembling talent, and getting your organization to reach consensus. Countless leaders have used clever techniques, including compensation plans, career incentives, intellectual bludgeoning, or Byzantine blackmail to build a team or drive it into agreement. None of these techniques is sustainable. And none of these helps you in the dark hour of choosing from among ambiguous or unpleasant paths. Expert application of the fours skills combined with some refinements, on the other hand, provides a sustainable platform for skillfully reaching agreements, assembling talent, and making the tough choices you inevitably will face.

> With a strong foundation and structure in place, you can harness your ambition toward something extraordinary.

Finally, we return to the guiding definition of leadership for this entire text. Leadership is a relationship in which you inspire and motivate others to make a sustained effort toward a common goal. This book assumes you already have determination, drive, and a desire to lead well. You have ambition. With a strong foundation and structure in place, you are then prepared to effectively harness your ambition toward something extraordinary—both in terms of its challenge and its scope. Don't settle for a comfortable objective. Don't settle for a purpose that serves only a few. Choose an ambition that is worthy of your time and effort, one that will leave a legacy of excellence on the people you influence, interact with, and inspire. Applying our house metaphor, it's only with a bold ambition that seeks to serve many and aims toward a grand challenge that you create a durable roof under which you can fully develop relationships and inspire others to work hard even in times of hardship and distress.

PART I

FUNDAMENTAL LEADERSHIP SKILLS

Listening

Storytelling

Negotiating

Assessing People

CHAPTER 4

LISTENING

We have two ears and one mouth
so that we can listen twice as much as we speak.

Epictetus[8]

Listening is by far the most important skill for a leader to hone. Have you ever seen a leader who seems unflappable and remains calm in even the most chaotic circumstances? Watch that person closely and you will see the secret to this cool demeanor—focused listening. As a leader, you need to pay attention to the words and actions of others while suspending judgment long enough to allow your intellect to catch up with your instincts. Why? If you speak too soon, you shut off creative impulse. You shut off collaboration. By speaking too soon, you force ideas on your team, even if that is not your intention. When you keep silent long enough to understand fully—not just hear—what someone is saying or doing, you create space for that person to invent, aspire, and contribute. By creating that space, you afford your team a sense of ownership, and you make room for the possibility that someone on your team has the best idea at this moment. By listening carefully, you sharpen all your sens and promote composure among those around you.

Pay Attention

There are many ways to listen; the most obvious is with your ears. However the act of listening is far more nuanced than just hearing words. To do it effectively you must pay careful attention to sounds and much more. The pace, breath, tone, and inflection of the voice all combine to provide the implied meaning, intentions, state-of-mind, and needs of the speaker. Reactions of your fellow listeners can also teach much. When you listen attentively, you shelve your own thoughts, and for a moment there is no judgment, no discrimination, no understanding. Only listening. When you listen deliberately, your mind—which is like a hyperactive dog pulling on a leash—soon starts barking with ideas, assumptions, interpretations, and decisions. If you can hold that dog off for a bit, you can listen with clarity, which leads to hidden insights. Insights that are very useful to a leader.

Listening is not for ears alone. When you practice listening, you sharpen your other senses—sight, smell, taste, and touch. When you listen carefully with your ears, you can sense tone and inflection, cadence and emphasis—all of which combine to provide insight into the meaning of the words spoken. When you apply that same level of attention with your sight, you might notice a flicker in the corner of an eye,

> Listening is not for ears alone.
> When you practice listening, you sharpen your other senses.

twitch in the corner of a mouth, a shift in stance—all of which combine to provide insights into meaning both overt covert. You develop a perception skill that few even know , let alone master.

Our wonderful human brain can simultaneously process observations made with all our senses. Listening as a practice sharpens that awareness automatically and leads to clearer perception of what is happening with the people on your team and in their environment. This clearer perception leads to competitive advantage because you can identify critical cues about intentions and motivations.

ARE YOU LISTENING?

Most schools don't teach listening. Neither do most parents. The closest we get to teaching children to listen is concentration games such as I Spy, Where's Waldo? and Memory Match Cards, which emphasize keen observation but not listening per se. Early in childhood, by the third grade in the communities I have seen firsthand, we move our kids' efforts toward serious academic pursuits, which usually involve more than a decade of frenetic preparation for scarce slots among top universities. As a result, we produce well-educated men and women with a singular need to demonstrate that they are the smartest person in the room, who vie to answer first, and who are not very practiced at listening. How many times have you come across this person in your career? Are you one of them?

Some kids growing up in this education system react to competition by becoming a class clown in an attempt to divert academic scrutiny or out of scorn for it. No listening there. Those who cannot compete in the "speed-answer-game" or the corollary "snarky-comment-game" often give up. For the daydreaming or socializing becomes a deeply ingrained h Listening loses out here, too. Other kids end up pu non-intellectual competition, usually focused on run retaining possession of a fast-moving ball. These mor youngsters might learn to listen to a coach, but if you have ever coached kids, you know they aren't usually listening; they just get skilled at looking as if they are.

In other words, education, development, and training in every country on earth are invested in sharpening competitive skills. This is indeed necessary for leadership, but it is not sufficient. I have spent much of my life perfecting a competitive instinct. I love competition, thrive on it, and believe it is the fuel that makes a democracy and capitalism possible. What I find disappointing is that in the midst of all the competitive juices flowing in academic, athletic, and professional endeavors, we neglect to develop the most important skill we will ever have—careful listening. It is the doorway to understanding our world and our place in it, and is the source of every great leader's strength.

> Listening is the source of every great leader's strength.

If this doesn't make sense, consider the fact that a professional baseball coach doesn't win by hitting a home run. A baseball coach wins by getting the team to function well and consistently over the course of nearly one hundred ninety games each season. He assembles a team that has the potential to win. There are key athletes on the team that can hit home runs when needed most. There are those who pitch well at the beginning or at the end of a game. There are others who field the ball well together and make brilliant defensive plays. To guide a team to victory, the baseball coach must have a very clear awareness of abilities, temperament, and condition of each member of the team, and an awareness of each of these critical areas is best developed by practicing clear and concentrated listening every day on and off the field. With a competitive drive, the coach will make the effort to lead the team well. And, if he listens well and pays attention with all his senses, the coach can consistently lead them to win.

LISTEN AND LEARN

Listening is a skill that, like any other, is mastered only through practice. And because listening isn't part of the standard primary or secondary curriculum, we are all sorely in need of practice. Our minds are very busy. You and I and every person trying to lead an organization has a mind that acts like a dog sniffing, chasing, and barking at shadows and leaves rustling in the breeze. Learning to listen meticulously is a lot like training a dog. Want to learn how? Let's practice.

Breathe. Find a quiet place. Sit still and comfortably with a reasonably straight but relaxed spine. Close your eyes. Bring all your awareness to your breath as you inhale and exhale as fully and deeply as you can. Allow your mind and body to relax and settle a bit as you use the breath to bring yourself into the present moment.

Observe. Open your eyes and look down at what is in front of you. With your eyes open, you are less likely to start daydreaming. For this practice to be effective, be sure to stay awake and present. What do you hear? Can you hear traffic? Birds chirping? People talking nearby? Your heartbeat? The blood rushing in your ears? A clock ticking? Your breath? Let your mind roam and listen to everything around you, all while your eyes are open.

Concentrate. With your eyes still open, concentrate on your slow, deep breaths in silence. Listen to each breath carefully as it enters your nostrils, passes through your trachea, fills your lungs, and then reverses. Continue to listen to the inhales, exhales, and subtle spaces in between. These sounds and the sounds of all the activity around you can each be perceived individually and collectively in each breath. Every time your mind wanders away from your breath, just smile, take an extra deep breath, and start again. You are concentrating on one point amidst all the activity around you. Just breathe. You are training your mind to sit still instead of roam.

Awareness. You may get bored listening to your breath. You might become frustrated that you end up in a daydream after each few breaths, even though your eyes are open. You might feel antsy. You might realize you are hungry. No matter what you experience, whenever you notice that you have strayed from your breath, you are having a spark of awareness—you just woke up. Use that awareness and just come back to studying each breath while you observe all the other sounds around you and in you. Practice patience with yourself. Practice calm control. Practice staying present. You are gently training your concentration to come back on command.

Practice. Do this for at least five minutes every morning or evening, whenever you are likely to consistently set time aside. If you enjoy this practice, do it for ten or fifteen minutes every day or try it for five minutes three times a day. After two weeks, apply your honed, concentrated listening to someone speaking to you. If you notice that your mind wanders, becomes bored, or starts coming up with ideas while that person is speaking, use that same spark of awareness to return to the speaker. Come back to their voice, just like you came back to studying breaths. With practice, you will notice that you aren't drifting as much, and you will start to see, hear, and feel cues you may never have noticed before.

LISTENING INSPIRES

Leadership is a relationship, and listening is essential to building successful relationships. When people are heard fully and completely, without interruption and without debate until they have finished their point, they are more likely to trust you. They are far more likely to be receptive to whatever ideas you would like them to consider—whether it is a request you are making of them or an opinion you would like to share with them.

Have you ever seen a leader checking email messages on a laptop, BlackBerry, or iPhone during a meeting? Are you one of those leaders? Not only is this enormously disrespectful, it is self-defeating. By not listening and observing, you miss the most valuable information you need to lead, and you simultaneously devalue the speaker and the others in the room. Pay attention to the people in the room or cancel the meeting. Listening isn't just about getting information you need; the act of listening is the primary tool you have to inspire and motivate others.

> When people are heard fully and completely, they are more likely to trust you.

It doesn't take much effort to become a more effective listener. Consistent practice is essential. If you start now, in a few weeks you will already be a more skilled listener than the majority of people on the planet. The average adult attention span has been conditioned by years of television and Web browsing to last only about twenty seconds.[9] So if you can focus your attention for five minutes, then you will be operating fifteen times higher than the average. Not a bad start. Even more valuable, by practicing calm listening every day, your demeanor begins to adjust. You begin to be more deliberate, even in the midst of noise and chaos. You will appear unflappable, which is always inspiring. Your natural levels of passion and enthusiasm will not be dampened—they will be more focused.

People will start to take notice and you will too. What are you waiting for? Try it right now. We are at the end of this chapter. It is a good time to take five minutes to practice listening.

QUICK CUES—LISTENING

Be still and silent.

Relax your mind and observe.

Use your breath to focus your attention.

Let go of expectations and judgments.

Stay present and focused on your breath.

Each time you drift from observing your breath, gently guide yourself back to it.

Do this, in silence, five minutes every day.

Apply this awareness to all situations.

CHAPTER 5

STORYTELLING

Drama is life with the dull bits cut out.

Alfred Hitchcock[10]

A once popular nursery rhyme begins "In fourteen hundred ninety-two, Columbus sailed the ocean blue. He had three ships and left from Spain. He sailed in sunshine, wind and rain." Indeed he did, but he did not travel alone. The sailors on the *Niña*, *Pinta*, and *Santa María* needed to firmly believe that their captain really knew a faster route to access the spice trades normally reached only by lengthy, treacherous voyages. They needed to believe he would get them to the East Indies despite a lack of good charts to guide their course across the Atlantic Ocean. It was a long journey of boring seas peppered by nightmarish storms, rumored death matches with whales and giant squid, and fears of traveling over the edge of the world itself. They were filled with excitement but also the anxiety that comes with voyaging into the unknown.[11]

Old Christopher Columbus knew how to spin a good yarn—he used storytelling to get the Spanish monarchy to finance his proposed journey beyond the edge of a flat world.

The Italian adventurer used storytelling to hire a crew without having a good map and to keep them from killing each other, even after the voyage took longer than promised. He told stories to keep the peace during times of confusion, and after he led the survivors home, he told more stories to hire yet another crew even though his first trip ended in the Bahamas instead of Malaysia—about ten thousand nautical miles off course. Columbus had to sell his vision through storytelling to groups of his men because he didn't get to interact with each crewmember on each of his ships during the long journey. His stories had to provide stamina, direction, and purpose to all three crews across months of hardship.

Cultivate Confidence

As you begin to lead larger organizations, you become like Columbus—farther removed from most of the individuals doing the work. As a practical matter, you are unable to listen to and engage each individual in a large organization. Storytelling becomes your most valuable tool for communicating the goals, values, and standards of the organization. In short, your ability to motivate and inspire is directly proportional to your ability to tell a good story.

Storytelling is a narrative that educates, explains, entertains, and conveys values and ambitions. It is a human activity shared in every culture. Storytelling is often used to make a point, but it can also be used to mislead. There can be truth in a story of fiction, and falsehood in a story filled with facts. Storytelling itself is neither good nor bad—it is your intention that is good or bad. Storytelling is vital to good leadership in any size organization. Your team doesn't need you merely to recite statistics, facts, or progress against milestones. You may need to provide that sterile information at times to inform, but your stakeholders—including staff, volunteers, chain of command, partners, shareholders, trustees, family, and friends—need you to give those facts meaning. They need context because it is only by relating the facts to the wider purpose that they cultivate their own faith in the mission, which leads to their inspired and sustained effort. It's only then that you're able to build relationships around a common effort.

People on your team want to believe in you as much as those sailors believed in Columbus. The vast majority of people want someone else to lead because they don't want the responsibility. This is part of what provides you the opportunity in the first place. And while you are leading them to wherever "there" is, you need to cultivate their confidence through storytelling—the meaningful narrative about their association with a worthy cause—

> Your ability to motivate and inspire is directly proportional to your ability to tell a good story.

because that is how they reassure themselves in the midst of chaos or doldrums that what they are doing matters. You need to remind them where they are going so they don't feel the urge to find a more meaningful mission elsewhere. Remember, for most people, incremental compensation carries far less weight than clarity of purpose.

Your team also needs to hear stories that celebrate progress, even if it is only a small progress such as sailing a hundred knots in a day, improving the throughput of a manufacturing plant by 1 percent, or finally winning one game in a long season of losses. This is especially true for those on your staff working on the most critical projects. If they are good, and you hope they are, then they are intensely focused on achieving personal milestones or improving individual performance and rarely have a clear view of the big picture in which their efforts reside. They need you to provide a context in vivid and believable detail by enthusiastically celebrating each element of progress toward the greater objective.

And of course, all human beings can relate to experiences that highlight your shared hard times and failures. When you tell those stories well, especially with some self-deprecating insights, you demonstrate that you are human and that you care about the same things they care about. You have the opportunity to reiterate how important it is that they don't give up because the purpose is clear and worthy of their continued effort.

Be Authentic

Leadership is relationship. And in every strong relationship, you need to convey effectively your enthusiasm, aspirations, and concerns. The critical factor for leaders is authenticity. How you tell stories, how often you tell them, and whether you strike the right balance among clinical-fact recitation, spellbinding oration, and pounding on the bully pulpit are factors you cannot formulate in advance. You develop the right style and rhythm for your particular situation only through practice. No matter what balance you do strike, however, to lead well, you need to be a good storyteller. Fortunately, it is a skill anyone can hone. You only need to make the effort.

Every time you speak, you are telling a story. I am telling you a story right now. As I write these words, my mouth is mumbling late at night while my wife sleeps next to me. I am testing tone and phrasing. My story for you has been captured in bytes, ink on paper, and finally stored in the form of this book for you. Want to practice storytelling? You already do it constantly but probably not consciously.

Do you like soccer? Basketball? How about fishing? Shopping? Still dreaming about finally owning that beautiful, fast car with stripes? Planning a long holiday? I can guarantee that if you have a passion, you have expressed an opinion about it, and in doing so, you have told a story.

Unless you live in a hermitage, someone is almost always asking you a question. Each question you encounter is an opportunity to practice storytelling. Don't just answer. Answer with flair. Experiment with different speaking styles. Feel free to mimic phrasing from your favorite comedian, actor, or preacher to see how it feels and how it is received. If it flops, toss it. If it works,

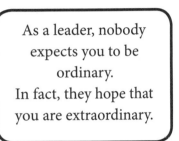

As a leader, nobody expects you to be ordinary.
In fact, they hope that you are extraordinary.

try it some more. When you answer a question, have the courage to say something colorful or expressive. Only then will you discover your authentic voice. Practice being spontaneous because almost nobody is. Most people are afraid of seeming out of place or saying something off base. You have permission to be decidedly un-average. As a leader, nobody expects you to be ordinary. In fact, they hope that you are extraordinary.

PUSH YOURSELF

You are going to be a good storyteller only if you test and push your creativity a little every day. The responses you get in those experimental moments build a sense of timing and phrasing that comes naturally when you have to stand in front of a large audience. When you face the pressure of a public speaking moment and the stakes are high, you won't have time to consciously plan timing and phrasing. The time to practice those elements is whenever you are asked a question. So think about what you are doing before you speak. As you encounter questions, decide how you are going to give compelling answers—and then do it.

Remember, leaders are not reporters. Leaders are actors. Use the tools of the theater. If you have no prior acting experience, you might consider taking an improvisational acting class. Meanwhile, if you are unwilling or unable to sign up for an improv class, consider every question you are asked an invitation to practice storytelling.

SPONTANEOUS STORYTELLING

- ❑ Be authentic.

- ❑ Let your emotions come to the surface because they convey meaning and credibility.

- ❑ Anecdotes and metaphors make new concepts easier to understand—try them and if they fail, declare out loud that they failed and enjoy a good laugh.

- ❑ There is unity in opposites. When you get stuck on how to answer a question or express an idea, think about the opposite, and it almost always unlocks the right phrase.

- ❑ Pause frequently and pace yourself —your audience needs time to digest your story in bits and pieces, and you need time to play off their reactions.

❏ Be expressive. Your audience receives only 7 percent of your emotions and feelings from your words—the rest you communicate through tone and movement.[12]

❏ Don't be afraid to exaggerate—just make sure it's clear that you are exaggerating.

❏ Always remember that you are speaking to an audience, and whether it is one person or a hall filled with several thousand, they want to hear what you have to say. Tell your story loud and proud.

Exercising Eloquence

You don't have to limit storytelling practice to getting up in front of an audience. You can practice storytelling privately with a simple, descriptive exercise now and then. Pick up any magazine or newspaper and flip through the pages until you find a photo that captures your attention. Study it in detail. Imagine yourself having just arrived in the photo setting and open all your senses. Then answer the following questions out loud, as though you were explaining it to a friend:

❏ What sounds are there?

❏ What does it smell like there?

❏ Can you taste anything in the photo? What flavors are there?

❏ What is the temperature? What does that feel like on your skin?

❏ If you were to take your shoes off, what would you feel on your toes right now?

❑ Are there any people in the photo? What do you say to them? What do they say to you?

You must practice this out loud if you want to train your mind and body to work together. If you do this in silence, it won't become muscle memory. Well-practiced silent mumblings won't help you when you take the stage or speak to a room full of people.

TREASURE HUNTING

Finally, you can practice by studying stories told by others. Pick the first appropriate person you see on any morning and ask him or her about the weekend, a recent trip, or some other event. Dig for sensory details. What colors? What sounds? What smells? Taste? Texture? Feelings? As your storyteller describes his or her experience in detail, make a mental note of any metaphors or exaggerations you really like. This is like digging for treasure. Repeat out loud anything you like or find powerful, right then and there. You could simply repeat the phrase, "You really think it felt like sandpaper?" Or you could add a reaction adding to a metaphor the person uses. If someone says, "The snow looked like icing on a cinnamon roll," you can respond with, "Cinnamon Roll. That makes my mouth water!" Verbalizing any expressions you notice and like will naturally lodge those phrases in your muscle memory, and you will be able to draw on them later when you have the opportunity to tell a story in public.

Stories Move Mountains

As you prepare for your next public speaking opportunity, consider telling a story instead of just reciting facts. If you aren't convinced that makes sense, consider what your stakeholders will remember when you are done. Will they recite your statistics, facts, and imperatives in a logical form, or will they remember and share your enthusiasm or disappointment, repeating your vivid, descriptive language?

In the summer of 1963, a young, African-American preacher faced a similar choice as he stood before a crowd that had gathered to assert their civil rights. He could have recited a logical and well-formed list of legal and social grievances, demanding that their situation be improved, and he would have received applause and cheers from many in the audience. That same young man chose, instead, to tell a story filled with metaphors, deliberate repetition, and sensory language that evoked emotions and emphasized the contrasting conditions he had witnessed. Take a moment to slowly read and benefit from some of his words—

> ...Five score years ago, a great American, in whose symbolic shadow we stand today, signed the Emancipation Proclamation. This momentous decree came as a great beacon light of hope to millions of Negro slaves who had been seared in the flames of withering injustice. It came as a joyous daybreak to end the long night of their captivity.

> But one hundred years later, the Negro still is not free. One hundred years later, the life of the Negro is still sadly crippled by the manacles of segregation and the chains of discrimination. One hundred years later, the

Negro lives on a lonely island of poverty in the midst of a vast ocean of material prosperity. One hundred years later, the Negro is still languishing in the corners of American society and finds himself an exile in his own land. So we have come here today to dramatize a shameful condition…

You might not recognize those brilliant words but you have undoubtedly seen and heard the end of this storytelling episode when the voice of Dr. Martin Luther King Jr. eloquently rang—

…we will be able to speed up that day when all of God's children, black men and white men, Jews and Gentiles, Protestants and Catholics, will be able to join hands and sing in the words of the old Negro spiritual, 'Free at last! Free at last! Thank God Almighty, we are free at last!'

Instead of merely acknowledging the crowd and their mission on that summer day, Dr. King told a story that has endured as an icon of brilliant oration for decades and continues to inspire many millions of people around the world.[13] You have the same tools he had when he wrote and told that story. You have eyes, ears, nose, tongue, body, and mind. You have ambition. You have wit. What he had in addition to all that was practice. Substantial practice. Every Sunday he served as a minister and spoke to his congregation, and every chance he had to speak about civil rights, he did so with passion and determination. In time, he honed his message and his delivery to perfection. You can be inspiring, insightful, and articulate if you practice. You cannot if you wait for someday to start trying. Start now. Please. Your organization is praying you get good at this.

QUICK CUES—STORYTELLING

Answer questions with flair—have fun.

Experiment with vivid descriptions.

Use emotions, anecdotes, exaggerations, and metaphors.

Pause, breathe, and observe reactions to your style, timing, and phrases.

Be authentic.

Consider every question you encounter as an opportunity to practice being descriptive.

CHAPTER 6

NEGOTIATING

Victor and vanquished
never unite in substantial agreement.

Tacitus[14]

My first manager and mentor, George, was a senior executive for a large telecommunications company. He was a brilliant negotiator. I watched him easily establish a commanding rapport with senior executives of Fortune 100 companies at a trade show, bargain confidently with shrewd Middle Eastern military and political leaders, and walk a factory floor addressing individual employees by name, easily persuading them to work long, hard hours on daunting projects.

As his young protégé, I eagerly studied George and one day asked him how he learned to be so persuasive, regardless of the situation. He said, "Everything in life comes down to two people negotiating in good faith. If you communicate clearly and sincerely, you can achieve anything." In twenty-five years I have not found one example to the contrary. Sales representative and buyer discussing terms. Cop and firefighter managing a crime scene. Teacher and principal developing a curriculum. Family doctor and surgeon at an emergency. Engineer and artist balancing the practical with the beautiful. Actor and director refining a scene. Entrepreneur and investor exploring options. So many combinations and permutations. Among all those pairings, whenever both parties reached agreement and were sincere and clear in their communication, a foundation of trust ensued and spread rapidly to others around them. Negotiation is the cornerstone of human relationships.

Naturally, I asked George how I could get good at this. "First, practice. Fail. Then, practice some more," was his droll answer. George was, of course, right. The errors in negotiation are rarely fatal, and as Nietzsche reminded us years ago, "That which does not kill us makes us stronger."

Negotiation is not just haggling. Haggling—also known as bargaining—is certainly a useful process for an occasional, significant transaction such as buying a car or selling a house, and it is the means by which two parties trade concessions until a mutual compromise is reached. Negotiation is more prevalent and is a foundation of leadership. It is a precise form of communication with a clear purpose—a process of coming to agreement about a future event you have a role in creating. Negotiation takes place almost constantly when two or more people are in one place.

It is obvious to anyone who has ever led a team that consistent success requires effective negotiation among the people on that team. When negotiation breaks down, the team's performance degrades quickly. Sometimes that poor team performance is evident in operational metrics such as revenues, milestones achieved, or objectives reached. More often, poor team performance is experienced as a lack of trust among the

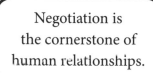

Negotiation is the cornerstone of human relationships.

members, and as a result, the problem is misdiagnosed. Instead of addressing negotiation skills, many teams have tried to overcome trust and other relationship concerns with team-building exercises such as softball games, bowling events, late night parties, professionally facilitated rope climbing courses, or personality discovery workshops.

These activities can develop emotional bonds among individuals on a team. They can also foster relationships with better communication. In my experience, however, none of these is a sustainable method for building negotiation skills and productive relationships because the lessons learned weren't applied in a work environment. For negotiation improvements in a team to hold in the long-term, they must be learned and applied in the practice of daily activity.

THE NEGOTIATION CYCLE

Almost a decade ago I learned a powerful negotiating protocol[15] that dramatically improved the function of my management team. We had inherited a brutal scenario: Our company was quickly running out of cash and the employees were demoralized. The executive team was under severe stress. But what began as a jumble of personality conflicts, confused commitments, and high frustration evolved quickly with the help of this system into a leadership team that drove planning, accountability, and achievement. After years of subsequent practice with this particular negotiation style and watching others apply similar approaches, I have settled on a three-part system that I have seen others implement with good success. Clarity is the key to this process. The three components of this effective approach to negotiating are making the request, making the commitment, and declaring the obstacle.

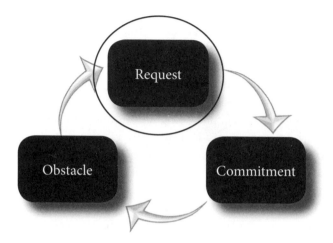

Making the Request

In most cases, negotiation failure stems from a lack of understanding between two people about a commitment being requested or made. Remember, negotiation is communication with a purpose—you are coming to agreement on the specifics of some future goal you share. The first element of an effective negotiation is making the request. You want something done, you need access to information, or you need the use of a resource. You ask for it. How you ask for it has a direct impact on the likelihood that you will get what you expect. Every request plants a seed of trust so you must be clear that you are requesting a promise. And you must be sure that the person receiving your request obtains a detailed understanding about what you want and when you want it. The clear request formula is:

I need (describe the action or deliverable in detail) **by** (be specific about the date). **Will you do that?**

To help illustrate, consider a very simple situation—you and a colleague are working late on a tight deadline. Your colleague notices how tired you look and offers to get you some coffee. You respond, **"Thank you, I'd love some coffee."** This request is not specific enough to ensure that you will get what you need. Do you want to get that coffee yourself or are you accepting your friend's offer to get it for you? Do you like it black or with cream? Do you like it with sugar, honey, cinnamon? Nor is it clear where and when you want that cup of coffee. Now? In an hour? Here? At the coffee maker? Elsewhere? A better request would be: **"Thank you; I'd love a big mug of hot coffee. If they have sugar and cream, please bring some with a spoon. I'll keep working on this until you get back and then we can both take a break. Thanks!"**

If there can be this much unspoken detail and potential ambiguity inherent in a friendly cup of coffee between colleagues, imagine how much more exists in the requests we make every day in our work. Requesting with precision is the first step to successful negotiation. After making the request, listen carefully. If you don't get a clear commitment, then you must ask for it. This might sound like a rigid method, but it works because it provokes and encourages the other person to reflect and respond clearly.

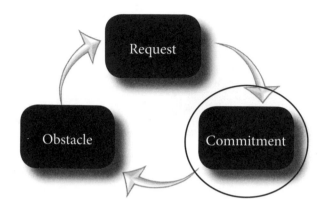

Making the Commitment

The second element of effective negotiation is making the commitment. You have been asked to do something, provide something, or deliver something. If you cannot follow through on what has been requested, just saying no isn't enough. Propose an alternative. If you do make a commitment, then you must be specific about what you will do and when. You must understand and consider the full scope of the request before you can commit and begin to create a bond of trust. If the request is fuzzy, you have an obligation to ask questions until it is clear. The clear commitment formula is:

I will (state the action or deliverable in your own words) **by** (date you are willing to commit to).

Going back to the sociable cup-of-coffee situation, responding to "Thank you, I'd love some coffee" with **"Sure"** is helpful but unclear. When the request is vague, you must ask for more information. How much coffee? How do you take your coffee? Would you like that now? Once you have all the facts, an effective response should be something like, **"Sure. I'll get you a big mug of coffee, some sugar, cream, and a spoon, and I'll be back in two minutes."**

This may sound a bit ridiculous given our simple coffee example—or it may sound a bit like being a barista at a coffee shop—but when this mirrored request and commitment protocol is applied to the complex requests that occur every day in every field of endeavor, including software development, curriculum design, event planning, manufacturing, crop harvesting, security operations, hotels, hospitals, and kitchens all around the world, you can see how it helps form a firm agreement based on clear, unequivocal communication.

A VARIATION ON COMMITMENT

Sometimes you just don't have enough information to make a commitment. What should you do? You are still obligated to commit because walking away is not an option in a long-term relationship. Instead, you must "commit to commit." Since you cannot respond to the request with a commitment now, you commit to a future time when you will make a specific commitment. For example:

I am sorry, but I can't be sure at this moment. Can I get you a commitment by (state your timeframe)?

Obviously there are other scenarios when the requested action or timeframe does not match what you can promise. Discussion and bargaining about what is reasonable ensues, but it is the obligation of the person making the commitment to promise only to what he or she can deliver with confidence and to express that level of confidence in precise terms. As the requestor, if you don't get that precision in both commitment and the confidence level, you need to ask for it. If you don't get the precision, you don't have a commitment. You have hot air.

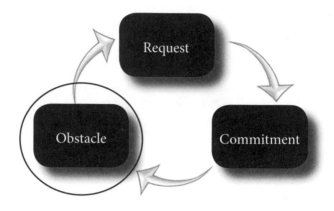

Declaring the Obstacle

The third, often neglected element, in negotiation is declaring the obstacle. A clear request has been made. A clear commitment has been made. The negotiating parties involved return to their busy schedules, away from one another. Something unexpected appears, and the commitment is at significant risk or is no longer possible as promised. It is the obligation of the one who made the promise to inform immediately the requestor that the promise is at risk or is no longer tenable. This is declaring the obstacle. With that declaration, both parties have a responsibility to discuss alternatives, given the new facts.

Many people skip this step in fear of being seen as weak or having failed to deliver. Failure to deliver doesn't breach trust. But failure to declare an obstacle does. Some people choose to be heroic and pull out all stops to deliver as promised. This approach is not sustainable, and worse, it misses the opportunity to create a shared understanding of the operating limits in which the team is functioning. You may still need to deliver as promised to help the team succeed in the mission at hand, but if you declare an obstacle, the requestor is aware of the risk and can make adjustments. Declaring an obstacle has two parts and takes this form:

1. **I am sorry, but my promise to** (detailed request in your own words) **by** (date you committed to) **is now at risk due to** (give explanation for what caused the obstacle).

2. **I need your help to resolve this issue** (Can we change the request details or timeframe? Can you help me eliminate or mitigate the cause of the obstacle?).

In our simplistic, collegial coffee-cup example you might say, **"I am sorry. I just found out the coffee maker is broken. Do you want to take a break and we can run to the coffee shop down the road, or if you'd like to continue working, can I get you a cup of black tea or a perhaps a can of Coke or Pepsi instead?"**

Are there situations when you wouldn't declare an obstacle? Rarely. If you are in a disaster cut off from all communication or if your failure to deliver on a commitment would cost the lives of others, then by all means, skip the obstacle declaration and go all out to deliver as promised. On the other hand, if you can communicate, you must make it known as soon as there is an obstacle, and you must propose an alternative commitmen Similarly, if failing to deliver will not cost the lives of your te then please declare an obstacle as soon as you encounter i

As the leader, you must foster a working environment in which a quick and solution-centered declaration of an obstacle is rewarded. You should also frown upon failure to declare obstacles. By creating an atmosphere in which obstacles are declared openly, you ensure that the entire organization learns its strengths and weaknesses and you ensure that your team communicates clearly with accountability.

> Everything in life comes down to two people negotiating in good faith.

Any two people who engage in this complete negotiation-cycle serve as a node of trust for the rest of the organization. Each pair is interwoven in a networked fabric with all the other pairs, and it is from this fabric of relationships that the organization derives performance. Failure to recognize this interdependency is one of the most common sources of friction and dysfunction on leadership teams. If this process sounds overly orchestrated, please try it for a few weeks, and you will see how well it works. As you continue to use it, you can infuse it with your own language and style, and it will quickly become second nature.

Lead by Example

If you practice this negotiation methodology and see its value firsthand, you may be tempted to impose it. But it's much better if you simply embody the protocol by making clear requests, making clear commitments, clarifying requests from others, and clarifying commitments from others. If you encounter an obstacle to a commitment you have made, declare ly and resolve it. If someone else declares an obstacle, use that scenario as a positive example for others to emulate. I have seen this negotiation protocol quickly adopted in multiple organizations just by way of leading by example.

This brings us back to George. He asserted that everything in life comes down to two people negotiating in good faith. As a leader, you are trying to get your team to achieve. To inspire and motivate your staff to make a sustained effort, you must build lasting relationships. Every request and every commitment is a chance to foster those relationships. Negotiation in good faith shouldn't be reserved for big deal-making moments. It takes place every day and is the cornerstone of human relationship. Your role as the leader goes beyond making clear requests or commitments. You must also assist others through probing inquiry. For example, if you hear an ambiguous request, help make it clear by asking questions. If you hear a vague commitment, clarify it by asking questions.

You may be wondering how to master this process. George already answered that. First, practice. Fail. Then, practice some more. So here is my request of you. I'd like you to practice this three-part protocol. Ask somebody for something right now. The taxi driver. The flight attendant. A person sitting near you. Anyone will do. Ask for something. Be precise in your request. Listen carefully to the response. Get a commitment. Clarify until the commitment is exactly agreed upon. Try it now.

QUICK CUES—NEGOTIATING

Everything comes down to two people negotiating in good faith.

Make clear requests and demand the same.

Make clear commitments and demand the same.

Declare obstacles immediately and demand the same.

Resolve obstacles together.

CHAPTER 7

ASSESSING PEOPLE

Everything that irritates us about others
can lead us to an understanding of ourselves.

Carl Jung[16]

Who sets the standard of excellence in an organization? The leader does. As a leader, do you spend significant time measuring results? Hope not! You are too late if that is what you are focused on. Are you investing considerable effort evaluating processes and procedures? You better not be. You aren't operating a machine; you are leading. While measuring results and improving processes are important functions of managing an organization, your highest priority as a leader is to inspire and motivate. To inspire and motivate, you must listen, tell good stories, and negotiate effectively, but above all, you must become a master at assessing people. Do you care about the people you lead? If not, you will fail. Perhaps not today, but your doom is inevitable. If you sincerely care about the people you lead, then you need to demonstrate that you value their effort and contribution. If you have accurately assessed the individuals on your team and adequately communicated those assessments to them, then you've shown them respect, you've demonstrat gratitude, and you've made clear how their effort makes your collective ambition possible, and the result is a team that will be motivated to measure and deliver results—better than you could ever do on your own.

To assess people you must carefully set standards of excellence and keep track of the accuracy of your judgments of individuals against those standards. You cannot become skilled at this if you don't practice. There is just no way around the school of scrapes and bruises on this element of leadership because it is as much art as it is science. It's like playing guitar. If you want to improvise while playing with other musicians, you must first perfect your scales. When you have mastered your scales, then you can stop thinking about them and play with heart and feel your way through a jam session with others. Practicing assessments develops your "ear" for good judgment, which helps your intellect stay in tune with your instinct, and allows you to make swift, accurate evaluations. The more frequently you practice making assessments, the sooner you will hit the mark in the first shot.

> To inspire and motivate, you must become a master at assessing people.

Effectively assessing people includes three key components. The first is establishing standards of behavioral excellence for your organization. Second is providing regular and consistent critical assessments—both praise and criticism—directly to the people with whom you interact. Last is setting an empirical standard of behavior for the entire organization. This means that how you set standards and how you communicate assessments against those standards will either reinforce or negate your efforts to motivate and inspire.

SETTING STANDARDS

In all organizations, results and achievements are derivatives of their people. To lead successfully, you must establish clear standards to determine whether the individuals on your team are adequate to serve each other and your organization's mission. Fortunately, there are only five qualities that you must assess in order to ensure you have a team capable of functioning at an exceptional level. You can easily make an argument for having more than the five listed here, but beware. It is imperative that you set, assess, and communicate standards with your team frequently and consistently. This is not a formal performance appraisal. This is a communication process that links to the negotiation protocol described earlier in this book. If you have too many standards to track, you will find it too cumbersome to continue and then will fail to communicate your standards at the most effective time—during the daily activity of your team. Before we examine how to set the standards, let's first define the five requisite qualities:

- ❑ Workmanship

- ❑ Curiosity

- ❑ Willingness to admit error

- ❑ Technical proficiency

- ❑ Leadership

Workmanship. Workmanship is the driven, purposeful attention to detail that stems from a sense of pride in your work. This quality is more important than passion for your product, service, or mission. Passion is nice, but workmanship is necessary. Why? Because the sense of pride that comes from work naturally leads to expediency and a pursuit of excellence. I would rather encourage a workaholic perfectionist to take a vacation than try to push a lazy person to make an effort. While you can encourage someone to work hard by way of economic incentives and peer pressure, it is nearly impossible to teach an adult to care about the quality of his or her work. In most cases, those who take pride in their work tend to put forth substantial effort regardless of incentives, peer pressure, or circumstance. Keep in mind also that your own workmanship must measure favorably against your standards of excellence if you expect it of others. If you have people on your team who demonstrate exceptional attention to detail, reward them publicly to serve as an example for the rest.

Curiosity. Curiosity is an asset healthy human beings have inherent in their brain function. You need people on your team who have retained their youthful curiosity about the world around them despite any challenging circumstances they may have experienced in life. These individuals are always asking why and find it difficult to accept an assignment without an explanation. The curious employees aren't necessarily combative—they are just driven to understand. It certainly may be harder to lead people like this, but they make you a better leader by forcing you to be thoughtful about your requests and objectives rather than merely relying on your authority to determine a course of action. The pithy French philosopher Voltaire[17] once said, "Judge a man by his questions rather than by his answers." I couldn't agree more.

As with workmanship, you cannot train curiosity. You can provoke and encourage it. You must be openly curious yourself publicly reward those who highlight implicit assumptions, cross-examine evidence, and who make the effort to collects before making a decision. In an environment of openly curious people, even the most timid are more willing to express insights and interests worth exploring.

Willingness to Admit Error. Sincerity is a helpful behavior, but an outright willingness to admit error is essential to building trust in an organization because failure leads to progress. You need people on your team who understand this and value the accountability that comes with it. Unfortunately, some people develop a fear of failure and in the process lose the ability to learn from mistakes. Retaining individuals who cannot admit error undermines your credibility and diminishes your ability to inspire and motivate. Teams quickly become dysfunctional if key contributors are not held accountable for their declarations, decisions, or actions that have a detrimental impact on the organization. You can allow individuals to repair, redress, adjust, and adapt—but you cannot allow them to attribute without cause an unexpectedly negative outcome to someone else. Either they step up or you ask them to step out. Of course, the same is true for you.

Technical Proficiency. It's not likely that you are a specialist in every field or function that comprises your organization. You must, however, study each area in sufficient detail to be a reasonable judge of proficiency. You must be a student of your team's expertise. Learn from them. Make them teach you. Then push them to learn more so that you can continue to learn from them. You don't need to have the best and brightest in every field on your team, but you must have people who aspire to be the best, have the aptitude, and who are willing to work at it. How many standards for technical proficiency do you need to create? One for every function that reports directly to y... They may have points in common, but each role is unique... deserves some study on your part.

Leadership. In a larger organization, you must determine whether the people on your team are good leaders. You can use a framework like the one in this book to evaluate leadership, but before you make that effort, perform a quick test. Remember the core definition in this book—leadership is a relationship in which one person inspires and motivates a group to make a sustained effort toward a common goal. When you assess a leader on your team, ask yourself: Do most of the people on that team understand and support their goals? Is there a sense of camaraderie on that team? Do they respect their leader? Does that leader have strong relationships with peers? If the answers are yes across the board, the probability is high that leader is fine and you can wait to assess his or her leadership skills more thoroughly and meticulously in a formal evaluation.

If you answer no to any of these questions, then it's time to move fast and dig deep to find out what specific leadership skills need to improve or determine if you need to find a replacement. You must move quickly because a marginally functioning leader will have a far greater impact on your organization than any individual contributor.

Make Them Your Own

Now that you understand these five essential qualities, you're ready to make them your own standards. For each quality, you need to establish a brief description of excellence, also known as a rubric. Begin by asking yourself how you define excellence in each of these qualities. If you have never done this before, you can easily establish a baseline rubric by interviewing a few leaders in your field. Inquire how they describe excellence for each of these qualities, then consolidate and adjust the description based on your own experience or instinct. It's sometimes helpful to list the name of someone whom you consider a particularly good example to serve as a reference point. In case you would like a starting point, I have included a sample rubric in the appendix.

Keep descriptions concise and meaningful. Once you have clearly defined and established these standards of excellence, begin revising each rubric based on your experience with them over time. This should not be something you do once a year. This should be an ongoing task you attend to regularly. As a best practice, you should engage the people you lead in an open and frank discussion about the rubric for excellence you have drafted for each of the five qualities. That private or group-setting discussion and debate will help you not only refine the standards but also, in the process of debate, communicate the standards for the organization and allow your people to internalize them. The process overall will deepen the relationships you need to lead effectively.

MAKING PRIVATE ASSESSMENTS

Now that you've defined your five standards, you're ready to assess your people against those standards. The first step is private. Make your assessments on your own without communicating them to anyone. One method of privately assessing the people on your team is allowing them room to fail or succeed. Not only is this a powerful learning mechanism for the organization, but it also is highly motivating for leaders on your team.

STAND BACK AND ASSESS

John and Ariel were arguing at a staff meeting about the best approach to negotiate a partnership with a very powerful and influential organization. As the CEO, John wanted to apply a gentle and conciliatory approach. He was certain this would yield a deal the company could live with even though he suspected it would also lead to a less economically valuable agreement. As the senior marketing executive, Ariel insisted that this particular partner only understood power and leverage and therefore the best approach was to negotiate with strident demands. John was almost certain his approach was best, but he allowed Ariel to proceed with her plan. He knew that if she was right, their company would win and win big. If she was wrong, John was reasonably certain he could re-enter negotiations directly and salvage the business relationship.

John decided to concede the argument and told Ariel, "You can do it your way. You may be right, and if you are, your approach will lead to the best outcome. If you are wrong, it will be a mess. I will be here if it blows up in your face; just know that it will be your mess I am cleaning up." Ariel agreed, quite sure she was right. She proceeded, led the team negotiating the deal, and surprised both John and herself at her audacity and tenacity during the process. Ariel closed the deal on terms John would not have dared to hope for.

is situation allowed John to assess Ariel's workman-
hnical proficiency as a negotiator, and her leadership
omplex process with high stakes. It allowed John to

demonstrate to the rest of the team how much he respected his executives' opinions and abilities. And in the end, John had a result that was better than if he had insisted on using his own approach.

When you assess your team, regardless of what events or circumstances you use as the fodder for the appraisal, you must begin with a private evaluation that utilizes your standards and considers how the individual you're assessing measures up to each one. I am not advocating that you replace your formal evaluation system with this five-point assessment tool. There is great value in formal, comprehensive performance appraisals every six to twelve months. Instead, I am urging you to realize that the people on your team need to know what the standards of excellence are in terms that connect directly to their daily activities. They need to know how they are doing now, not a year from now. You must generate and deliver fresh assessments based on current activity. Making private assessments gives you the time and freedom to be thoughtful about those assessments before communicating them to the individuals on your team.

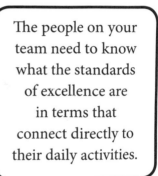

The people on your team need to know what the standards of excellence are in terms that connect directly to their daily activities.

SHARING ASSESSMENTS

Once you have set standards and have begun thoughtfully and privately assessing the people on your team, it's time to share those assessments—both praise and constructive criticism—with your staff. Frequent assessments in the form of acknowledgement or requests harness the power of small, incremental adjustments to behavior and also indicate that you care about the work they are doing. Nothing motivates more effectively. Frequent, regular "bite-sized" assessments are essential to your relationship with each member of your team and, if avoided or mishandled, can wreak havoc on everything you do as a leader.[18]

Deliver Powerful Praise

First, you must sincerely acknowledge each person's contribution, which is especially necessary to sustain motivation during challenging times. It's not difficult to do and doesn't require a lot of effort or expensive gifts or bonuses. A simple email expressing your gratitude is enough most of the time. And a handwritten, personal card carries immense value these days.

Building Goodwill

Mary was president of a successful small technology company. She knew everyone by name and even knew many of their families and loved ones. Mary had been a successful track athlete in her youth and briskly walked the halls with a smile. To make her employees laugh or groan, sometimes she would say outrageous things like "Did you sell anything today?" or "My coach always said, 'Run till you puke!' Why aren't you puking?" Each week she would publicly—in front of her entire company of one hundred people—acknowledge one employee's efforts. Sometimes it was a secretary who worked long hours on a proposal. Sometimes it was a salesperson that landed a new account.

Sometimes it was an engineer who worked tirelessly to solve a technical problem for a client.

Every week Mary also left at least one personal note of gratitude for someone who was working on a project of importance to her. Her employees had come to expect these little notes and valued them very highly, almost competitively sharing them with each other and good naturedly bragging about them at lunch breaks and company events.

The company suddenly encountered a severe cash flow crisis when larger competitors drove prices down at the same time that distribution costs were rising substantially. Mary's small company was trying to recover but did not have enough capital to survive until her distribution contracts could be renegotiated. She assembled her employees for their weekly meeting, explained the financial issues, answered questions, and then made an unusual request. "I am trying to avoid layoffs, but it's clear after cutting other expenses and delaying payments that we will not be able to make the full payroll," she said. Employees were stunned in silence.

She continued, "I cannot make you do this, but if we were able to collectively take a temporary pay cut for three months, we have a good shot at surviving this mess. If we don't voluntarily cut payroll expenses, we'll be forced to resort to layoffs." Whispers began to fill the room. Mary concluded with, "I will take no salary during these three months, and my execs have each agreed to take at least a 50 percent pay cut. Please let me know by the end of the day if you can contribute to this plan." By the end of that day, every employee met with Mary or one of her executives. Every single employee contributed at least a little to the voluntary pay cut, some very aggressively. The company made it through the crisis: Everyone's job was retained, everyone's pay was restored, and in a few months, everyone's sacrifice was retroactively paid. Poignantly, when the crisis was over, every employee taped a personal note to Mary's door, covering it with sentiments of gratitude and amazement.

In my experience, 80 percent of employee morale and retention issues are related to lack of recognition. Only 20 percent of employee morale issues are related to compensation. Your sincere, public recognition of the accomplishments, contributions, and efforts of your staff sets a clear standard of excellence. It also sets the standard for the leaders in your organization. You don't have to praise in public, but it helps to do so because it's better than cash, as Mary learned directly. And it fosters the relationships that the success of your organization depends on.

> Your sincere, public recognition of the accomplishments, contributions, and efforts of your staff sets a clear standard of excellence.

TELL THEM YOU NOTICED

Remember, as you provide positive feedback, it isn't only for the big wins. It's as simple as saying "thank you" now and then for something as small as a favor or a little extra effort. You are building relationships one brick at a time:

- ☐ If you have something good to say, don't delay.

- ☐ Be specific and don't fake it. The only thing worse than no praise is insincere praise.

- ☐ Connect your comments to the standard you are assessing. Provide context.

- ☐ Thank your people and encourage them to keep up the good work.

- ☐ Praise publically when you can. It reinforces and inspires.

- ☐ Notes, emails, voicemails, brief in-person comments work equally well.

MAKE EFFECTIVE CRITICISMS

Things aren't always coming up roses. Every now and then people will fail to live up to the standards you have set for workmanship, curiosity, willingness to admit error, technical proficiency, and leadership. Now and then you need to provide criticism.

Is there ever a good reason to criticize in public? If you said yes, you are wrong. Criticizing in public is tantamount to rule by fear. Niccolò Machiavelli is still infamous five hundred years after writing *The Prince*, and in the centuries since it was published, that "better-feared-than-loved" treatise has been shown time and again to be a failed philosophy. Only those who cannot go elsewhere will stay in an organization that is ruled by fear. And those who cannot leave are inspired to insubordination.

COUNTERPRODUCTIVE CRITICISM

Joel was a young, enthusiastic and driven entrepreneur. His intellect was formidable, and his education and professional pedigree impeccable. As he formed his company, he easily attracted talented and technically skilled people to join his mission. Although he had substantial business experience, Joel had never formed or run a company before. He had led teams, but always under the direction of seasoned leadership in a larger organization.

As a new CEO, Joel had to establish priorities and timelines. He relied on the only approach he trusted in this new situation—dictatorship. He decreed specifications, priorities, and timelines. Joel did not share his logic, his insights, or explain why some priorities shifted. This caused many of his most talented employees to feel objectified and emasculated. They argued for more visibility into the logic of projects, sequence, and priorities, and for the first time in his career, Joel sensed a looming loss of control.

He responded by prescribing even more precisely and lacing his instructions with public displays of anger, frustration, and accusations of insubordination, lack of commitment, and laziness. Nearly 60 percent of the employees quit within ten months. A few of the remaining employees contacted the board of directors and complained bitterly, causing the board to reprimand the CEO, demand a corrective action plan, and quietly begin recruiting a replacement.

In the many organizations I have led and observed, public criticism has consistently been counterproductive. It takes only one public criticism to wipe out goodwill built over months or years. Public criticism is one of the most damaging and demoralizing habits of men and women in power. And it is absurdly self-defeating. This isn't a rarified, graduate-level physics or psychology concept. You already understand that criticizing

> It only takes one public criticism to wipe out goodwill built over months or years.

in private allows a person time to react, digest, and respond reasonably. If your goal is to modify behavior or mitigate damage to the rest of the organization when you make a change on your team, your criticisms must be in private.

Making a Sandwich

For every criticism, you need to make sure you offer at least one positive comment before and after your critical feedback. It's often called "the sandwich" or a "praise-criticize-praise" formula. Tell people something they are doing well, then constructively explain how they aren't living up to standards, and then tell them you have confidence in them based on something they are doing well. The sandwich is easy and mitigates headaches, litigation, and repercussions in the rest of the organization.

For example, you might start the sandwich with something like:

"Bill, thanks for your hard work on Project Mercury last week. We made a lot of good progress."

After pausing, you progress to the meat of the matter:

"Bill, I need to talk to you about your failure to declare an obstacle on that project. I need you to step up and let me know any time a commitment you make isn't achievable. What is stopping you from doing that?"

After listening, vetting any assumptions, and clarifying what is going on, you can combine making a request with the last piece of the sandwich:

"Bill, I appreciate your good work on this project. You are an important part of the team. I need you to commit to declaring obstacles from here on—every time, no exceptions. Can I count on you?"

BE DEMANDING *AND* CONSTRUCTIVE

Remember, as you provide constructive criticism:

- ❑ Always communicate privately and in person or on the phone, never by email or on voicemail.

- ❑ When you need to criticize, don't procrastinate.

- ❑ Be specific and calm. Connect your comments to the standards you are assessing.

- ❑ Pause. Allow the criticism to be digested.

- ❑ Make a request for a specific commitment to change.

When you set clear standards, assess your people consistently against them, and share your assessments effectively, you combine all the elements of leadership we have discussed so far. You listen carefully. You publicly share successes stories, usually with a brief narrative story. You negotiate requests and commitments and obstacles. And in the end, you complete the foundation of the relationship in which you motivate and inspire a group of people to make a sustained effort toward a common goal. We have now covered the four fundamental skills; it's time to move on to Part II—the four essential functions of leadership

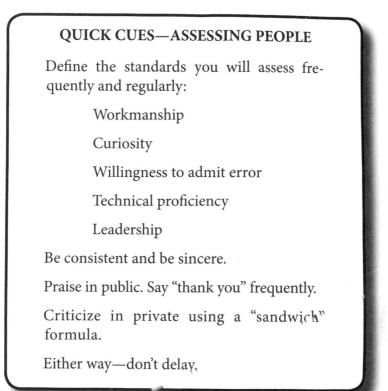

QUICK CUES—ASSESSING PEOPLE

Define the standards you will assess frequently and regularly:

> Workmanship
>
> Curiosity
>
> Willingness to admit error
>
> Technical proficiency
>
> Leadership

Be consistent and be sincere.

Praise in public. Say "thank you" frequently.

Criticize in private using a "sandwich" formula.

Either way—don't delay.

PART II

ESSENTIAL LEADERSHIP FUNCTIONS

Assembling Talent

Reaching Consensus

Making Tough Choices

Harnessing Ambition

CHAPTER 8

ASSEMBLING TALENT

There never were in the world two opinions alike,
no more than two hairs or two grains;
the most universal quality is diversity.

Michel de Montaigne[19]

Y ou need people to accomplish your mission. Without people to lead, you are the lonely, exhausted man or woman working at a flooding river's edge, singlehandedly building a dam from a wagonload of sand and a pile of empty bags as you try to save your house from being washed away. Valiant, maybe, but against the full force of nature it is a fruitless effort without the strength of others to join you in the monotonous and sweaty toil of shoveling sand, filling bags, lifting them into place, and re-supplying even more sand and bags.

If you wish to lead, you need people to follow you and work with you. How do you attract people to your mission? The same way you would get people to help you lift sandbags if you were at that flood—enlist people through your relationships. How do you then select from the people who appear at your door? The same way you choose from among those who would help you lift sandbags—you evaluate those who arrive and then combine their skills, their relationships, and their efforts to make the most of what you have.

RELATIONSHIPS ARE THE SOURCE

You will always need to attract talent, regardless of how long your organization has existed or how well-established it may be. It never stops. Your organization will need people with new skills and experiences as it expands in scope or size, and as your marketplace or environment shifts, you need to adapt your staff. In these frenetic days of the twenty-first century, you cannot expect that even the most loyal people on your team will be there until the mission is achieved. You will always need to draw new talent.

This does not mean hiring a recruiter. Recruiters can be helpful and even necessary at times to manage a hiring process, but you only need a recruiter to attract talent if your leadership has failed. Consider this in the context of the core definition of leadership used throughout this text—leadership is a relationship in which you inspire and motivate. It is quite obvious that you need to motivate and inspire your staff, your squad, your volunteers, your employees, or your constituents. An inspired and motivated staff eagerly spreads the word about the value of being on your team, which brings the best and brightest to your door. In other words, if you lead your team well, others will clamor to join you.

> You only need a recruiter to attract talent if your leadership has failed.

It might be less obvious in this particular context that you must also inspire your chain of command. Depending on your field or industry, your chain of command might be your board, your manager, your superior officer, or your sponsors. An inspired and motivated chain of command will promote your organization as a role model, making your organization a desired destination for those seeking superior leadership. Finally, you must also build strong relationships with peers in your field and your community. Peers who value their relationship with you will speak highly of your organization, which also drives talent to your team. Your relationship with your stakeholders—including superiors, subordinates, and community—determines what kind of talent you attract and therefore what kind of team you can assemble.

ATTRACTING TALENT

What skills do you need to build strong relationships with all these stakeholders in order to pull talent towards you? We have already covered them in the book thus far:

❑ **Listening.** This is one of the most important skills of an effective leader. Paying careful attention to all sensory cues enables you to be aware of talent when it becomes available, allowing you to surpass organizations whose leaders are not as attentive.

❑ **Storytelling.** You must be able to convey your organization's values and goals to many people at once. Well-told, concise stories about your team's hopes and achievements are widely disseminated, which means your ability to inspire and entice talent is extended well beyond your immediate audience in any given moment.

❑ **Negotiating.** Your ability to make clear requests, make clear commitments, and declare obstacles as they occur is the cornerstone for building lasting relationships. This skill motivates your team and generates respect among competitors and partner organizations—both sources of great talent.

❑ **Assessing People.** Your ability to evaluate people accurately, consistently, and honorably encourages your staff to remain on board even during difficult times, which is a strong signal of confidence for the more talented people who are considering your organization as a next step in their career.

If you master each of these skills and pay attention to the relationships you are forming with your stakeholders, you will naturally attract talent. When practiced daily and mastered over time, these skills generate a forceful current that brings talent to your door. Leadership is not a one-time event. It is an on-going series of actions spanning months or years. How you conduct yourself today as you employ these key skills will greatly impact your ability to attract talent tomorrow.

It is worth noting that there is one factor can draw talent regardless of skill—superior results. Even the most incompetent leader can attract talent if the organization is generating exceptional results. Of course, that same marginally skilled leader will struggle to retain valued workers or attract more talent once his or her fame and fortune wanes a bit. This has been particularly easy to see in the rapid boom and bust cycles in the technology sector. Companies such as Commodore Computer, Lotus, and Prodigy were consistently hailed as mighty forces while in their few years of glory and are now nearly forgotten, replaced by other more adaptable, more creative companies, some of whom are now already being replaced by yet another generation of nimble innovators. Compare their stories to Microsoft or Apple Computer, who continue to ebb and flow and thrive as though they feed on the high velocity turmoil of this challenging industry. Your field of endeavor may move more slowly, but if you are counting on superior results to attract talent, you are skating on thin ice. You need to master the fundamental skills of leadership if you want to attract and retain talent in your organization.

> If you are counting on superior results to attract talent, you are skating on thin ice.

CHOOSING THE RIGHT TALENT

Suppose you have talented, motivated people knocking on your door. How do you choose from among them in order to construct a cohesive team? I have worked in many organizations that conducted fist pounding in the executive suite with shouts of "We will only accept 'A' players on this team." Whenever I pushed those same executives for a definition, they would inevitably identify a sports star as a metaphor, as if that should make it obvious to me. Can you imagine a basketball team with only Kobe Bryant and Kobe Bryant wannabes? Can you imagine a soccer team with only Pelé clones? Can you imagine a high school staffed only with Albert Einstein doppelgangers? Even if you somehow think that makes sense, do you really think it's possible?

Attracting highly skilled individuals is useful for building a winning team, but technical proficiency, even brilliant technical proficiency, is not sufficient. You can combine the very best in every area of responsibility in your organization, but unless your team functions well together, you will fail to create sustainable value. A winning team is composed of many different players. We've already explored the need for a minimum level of technical proficiency you need to establish for your organization, and you need to assess individuals against the rubric you created for that standard. The question at hand is whether you need the very best in each functional area of your organization. The answer is no. Camaraderie and respectful dissent is more important than superb individual skill. In a competitive environment, you will lose to teams with far less education, experience, or even talent if they have excellent working relationships and discipline while your team does not.

DISCIPLINE DEFEATS TALENT

La eMe. Since the 1950s, intelligent, seasoned, hard-working cops throughout California have collected evidence with poor coordination and rarely agreed upon roles and responsibilities with the Federal Bureau of Investigation. As a result they have been repeatedly outflanked and outwitted by the relatively uneducated but ruthlessly focused and loyal La eMe gang, which has amassed over fifty thousand members across the United States as of 2008 and still operate a very profitable drug trafficking and extortion business.[20]

The English. At the Battle of Agincourt in 1415, a vastly outnumbered and nearly exhausted English force of six thousand men defeated a heavily armored and well-rested veteran French force of nearly fifty thousand. The French nobles led the attack with hubris, fully expecting a brief and glorious rout. Using a disciplined sequence of longbow and hand-to-hand tactics, the English killed many of the French mounted nobility, leaving their forces in disarray, arguing and competing with each other about the next move while the English continued to cut them down. The English won the battle and lost only five hundred men while the French suffered devastating losses.[21]

Google. AOL dominated the Internet advertising industry by late 1999 and was filled with brilliant engineers and business executives. Yet after its merger in 2000 with the equally powerful and successful Time Warner, the executive teams became mired in one-upmanship and self-preservation. By 2004, AOL lost its advertising dominance to Yahoo, whose leadership team was itself becoming mired in a byzantine array of competing interests. By 2007, Yahoo lost its dominance in online advertising to the innovative, focused, highly disciplined Google.

Diversity Is the Key

Building a team that functions well is essential in any field of endeavor. What is the single most important factor in creating a successful team? Diversity. For the purpose of this text, the word is used in a general sense—a diverse organization includes people who possess distinct qualities and experiences. Diversity is essential to your success as a leader, but it is not limited to gender and race, which is what most people think of when they hear that word. The principle of equal rights has justly demanded we focus on those elements, but as important as gender and race are in forming a strong team, a mix of education, learning styles, and professional experiences is also crucial. People with diverse backgrounds help you avoid relearning lessons that are old hat in one organization or community yet unheard of in yours.

MULTIDISCIPLINARY CRISIS

The AIDS pandemic serves as an instructive example of the need to combine talent from multiple disciplines in order to tackle a complex challenge. While the emergence of HIV that led to AIDS in the mid 1980s was a medical crisis, addressing the impact of AIDS was not strictly a medical challenge. To halt the spread of HIV and thereby reduce cases of AIDS requires a combination of biological research, sociological expertise, political leadership, public policy support, communication skills, educational systems, and both private and public investment. These disciplines were combined effectively in North America, where in 2007 less than 0.5 percent of the population was living with HIV and a much, much smaller percentage was newly infected that year.

Meanwhile in Sub-Saharan Africa, where these necessary disciplines are not as effectively combined, in 2007 nearly 3 percent of the population was living with HIV and almost two million people were newly infected in that year alone. An even more devastating comparison is the mortality rate of infected people in the two regions. In the United States, a little more than 1 percent of HIV-infected patients died from AIDS in 2007. In Sub-Saharan Africa, a stunning 7 percent of the HIV population died from AIDS that same year.[22]

The value of an effective, multidisciplinary effort is beneficial not only in a pandemic. Every organization of more than a few people is sufficiently complex to benefit from broad diversity in skills, backgrounds, and personality traits. Most teams have five to ten members. Too few, and the capacity to plan and build is limited. Too many, and reaching consensus becomes thorny. But even in a small team of only four or five people, diversity is achievable and is more valuable to the team than individual skill levels. Skill always improves linearly at the rate in which any one member of your team is willing and able to learn. Diversity, however, can impact your team exponentially by the addition of only one person with a different educational foundation, professional background, or learning style.

> Diversity is essential to your success as a leader, but it is not limited to gender and race.

For example, if your team has the typical collection of left-brained, analytically astute, milestone-oriented people, you can easily imagine how much more colorful and challenging the discussions would become if you added a right-brained, experimental, creative peer to the team. Instead of merely evaluating variances against a plan, you will find yourself debating whether the plan is any good. Of course, the inverse is also true. If you have a team of right-brainers, adding a left-brained member will change the conversation dramatically. Indeed, you might find it frustrating to add a new and dramatically different person, but if he or she helps stimulate a respectful debate, it is always useful and leads to informative and sometimes enlightening insights for you, your one-brained team, and the other-brained newcomer.[23]

Sad but True

Having made the point about diversity being more than just about gender and race, it's worth mentioning how important those two factors are. It's been a laughably sad experience to have attended decades of executive meetings in different organizations, filled with similarly wealthy, slightly overweight, over-40-year-old men. The rude jokes about women and minorities are always the same. The competitive banter about golf, college hoops, or football trivia remains the same. The approach to problem solving by calling upon one of their chosen golden boys is the same. I was once one of those boys touted as problem solver and the next generation of leadership. Even as I benefited from their confidence, I found the déjà vu experiences in the executive suite—in different countries, different industries, and different decades—rather eerie. In Europe, Asia, and the Middle East, senior executives discussed different sports and different ethnic groups served as the butt of jokes, but otherwise the dynamic remained the same. Same old crew comes up with the same old answers.

It has been instructive to see that each time one of these categorically homogeneous teams was forced by circumstance or a progressive leader to add a woman or a minority into the mix, the conversation changed permanently. After the inevitably awkward adjustment period passed—the old jokes and epithets weren't so smart anymore—new ideas and solutions to problems were proposed and implemented.

BUCKING THE STEREOTYPE

Molly was a shrewd, well-educated Jewish woman who grew up in Newton, a suburb east of Boston, which gave her an unmistakable accent and turn of phrase. She worked for a large, successful technology company that had operations on every continent and had customers in just about every country on earth. For nearly ten years, Molly served as a contract administrator in the United States and Europe. She was highly regarded in the company and the industry as tough, fair, and extremely capable of navigating thorny contractual negotiations.

The company had successfully served the government of Kuwait for many years as a supplier of equipment and services but suddenly encountered challenges with one of the contracts—the company and the customer had different interpretations about specifications required for payment. Millions of dollars were at stake. Senior management had tried for months to negotiate a resolution but had failed.

One of Molly's co-workers was serving as an analyst to the senior leadership and suggested that what they needed was Molly. The president guffawed at the naivety of that suggestion and pointed out that sending a woman to Kuwait was unthinkable, sending a Jew even more ridiculous. He stressed that sending a Jewish woman to serve as the company's representative in the negotiation might get her thrown in jail and would cost the company its standing in that country and possibly the entire region. Undaunted, the co-worker said, "Well, you have been trying for months and failed. If you continue to fail, you lose the money and likely the next contract. So at this point, what do you have to lose in asking Molly what she thinks?" After another month of failed attempts and more badgering from the co-worker, the president finally asked Molly if she was willing to take what might be a personal risk and most certainly was a professional risk to lead the negotiations.

She nearly jumped at her good fortune and the opportunity for adventure. Molly flew to Kuwait City with the otherwise all-male executive team. The Kuwaitis were stunned at her audacity and were also amused with the novelty of dealing with a Jewish woman instead of the usual team but were soon swayed by Molly's skill, good sense of humor, and negotiation brilliance. After several tense weeks of discussions and compromises, she led the company to the exact resolution that the executive team had unsuccessfully attempted for months by applying almost the same approach that her male predecessors had used. The difference was that Molly was an unusual and interesting character, and she was in fact a gifted negotiator. After the payments were arranged, the Kuwaitis requested that Molly be permanently assigned to the account. She successfully served in that region for years.

DELIBERATE TRANSFORMATION

The addition of just one person of a different gender, race, culture, ethnicity, professional background, educational foundation, or learning style can make the difference between a team that merely functions and a team that wins. Your team can hone and refine skills for years and make incremental improvements. Add one markedly new person to the team, and you create a transformational dynamic with exponential results.

There is, however, a word of caution on diversity. Leaders tend to surround themselves with people they admire and enjoy. As a result, leaders tend to select from a limited palette—consciously or not. Diversity on your team usually appears only if you deliberately choose to focus on it.

MERGING TALENT

Once you've attracted talent and made thoughtful choices in order to create a diverse mix of people of different genders, cultural backgrounds, professional experience, and learning styles, you must bring them together to function as a team. With many different styles, backgrounds, opinions, and vocabularies based in experience, there is always friction when coming together even if everyone is

Add one markedly new person to the team, and you create a transformational dynamic with exponential results

passionate about the same mission or objective. There is an old rhyme, accredited to Bruce W. Tuckman, that clarifies the typical pattern that a group dynamic tends to follow. It is:

Forming—Storming—Norming—Performing.

Several revisions and additions have been attached to this formula, but for the vast majority of leaders, this original, easy to remember pattern works very well as a guide. Based on my own experience, I suggest applying this abbreviated version of the model:

❑ **Forming.** This is the period when members are added to the team. Even adding just one new person to an existing team starts this process. There is considerable effort in nesting, organizing, reading the landscape, and laying low in the weeds while taking note of organizational risks and opportunities. It's the quiet before the storm.

❑ **Storming.** This is when differences are debated. It is in this heat that the different elements on your team combine, and if you pay close attention to negotiations and assessments, you can form new alloy from those disparate elements, stronger and more versatile than the individuals alone. You can also lose people with a weaker constitution in this stage.

❑ **Norming.** As the team sorts the good, the bad, and the ugly on everything from style to skills to expertise, the behavioral standards you have established through listening, storytelling, negotiating, and assessing people begin to be internalized by each of the members. The team starts to form its own rhythm.

❑ **Performing.** After behavioral norms are established, you can more easily align objectives and goals, and finally the team can begin performing—delivering results and driving the organization toward the common goal.

Unfortunately, you cannot avoid this merging process which occurs with every collection of human beings who are working together. It is in our nature since we are all social creatures. This group dynamic has always reminded me a great deal of the five stages of grief developed and published by Dr. Elisabeth Kübler-Ross: denial, anger, bargaining, depression, and acceptance. Grief not only is about death, birth, divorce, or other dramatic events; it also surfaces with any disruption to our life. Human beings simply don't take well to change. An individual goes through the five stages of grief any time there is a loss of any size, including a loss of routine, loss of existing balance of power, loss of clarity in job description, and so on. Adding a new team member causes each individual to go through a grief process, no matter how light or brief, and the summation of all those grief processes in a team seems to take on the collective pattern of *Forming—Storming—Norming—Performing.*

There is good news in all this. Each event in each stage of the team-merging process serves as an opportunity for you to practice and tune your leadership skills of listening, storytelling, negotiating, and assessing. If you practice these skills deliberately and transparently, explaining to your team where you think you are in the merging process and declaring what you are doing to be helpful in that moment as a result of your evaluation, then you open the conversation for others to make judgments about the state of the transition and their role in it. With this open approach, you cannot help but embody listening, storytelling, negotiating, and assessing people, and in the process you and your team quickly adopt the best practices among you. In this way, rather than suffering though the stages of team-merging and collective grief, you drive your team from the *Forming* stage into the *Performing* stage through an open collaboration of diverse talents, skills, and experiences that merge into one ambitious group.

QUICK CUES—ASSEMBLING TALENT

Your actions today create your talent pool tomorrow. Be sure to:

Listen well

Tell good stories

Negotiate effectively

Assess people honorably

You always need to attract talent.

Diversity is the key to a winning transformation.

Forming—Storming—Norming—Performing is necessary and useful for merging talent.

CHAPTER 9

REACHING CONSENSUS

*He who has learned to disagree without being disagreeable
has discovered the most valuable secret of a diplomat.*

Robert Estabrook [24]

Since your primary purpose as a leader is to inspire and motivate a group into sustained action toward a common goal, how do you get people to agree on a common goal? You can certainly impose your will and authority and declare the goals for your organization. Many leaders have done so, with some success. Are you sure you know the right goals? You probably have some really good ideas, but leadership is not a solo performance. You are trying to inspire and motivate others to work hard. By creating an open forum for the exchange of ideas in your organization, you are able to forge agreements and build the relationships that make consistently successful leadership possible.

You need your team to function well and start achieving results now, not in the distant future. For that to happen you need a collaborative environment that leverages your team's expertise, insights, and abilities. To foster that environment you must listen more than you speak, and you must avoid making assertions until absolutely necessary. You need your team to think, to aspire, to create, and if you are deliberate about your approach, they will come up with goals and plans better than you could have conceived on your own.

Listening is paramount in unifying the team. Please do not underestimate its value. As a leader, the instant you speak, two-thirds of your team stops thinking. This hefty first cohort will capitulate and begin to interpret or outright solicit your instructions. And of the remaining one-third still thinking, half of them will disagree with you just because you're the boss. They might not say so out loud, but you can count on them undermining your efforts when you aren't present. Time and time again over more than two decades, I have seen leaders speak too soon and lose the creativity, enthusiasm, and passion inherent in their team.

> The instant you speak, two-thirds of your team stops thinking.

In order to illustrate an effective method for reaching consensus, let's consider three distinct approaches. Each of these appears frequently among leaders attempting to align a team around objectives. To help you remember them, I've assigned each model a well-known character as a mnemonic device: Moses, Donald Trump, and Socrates.

THE MOSES MODEL

Our first archetype is Moses, also known as the Prince of Egypt, author of the Torah, and heroic figure revered throughout much of the world. He serves as a fine cautionary tale for leaders. Moses "went up into the mountain" and encountered God, who taught him *The Law* and asked him to present it to his followers. If you are familiar with the story in Exodus, you may remember that things didn't go so well for Moses when he came down from that mountain. Despite having a genuinely divine inspiration, Moses had significant trouble convincing his followers that the commandments he had on stone tablets were in fact *The Commandments* dictated by God Himself. While he was up in the mountain speaking with God, his followers had developed some ideas of their own. It took many arguments, some tragic deaths, a few miracles, and several decades of wandering in the wilderness before the people finally agreed to the goals and methods for life that Moses had presented on behalf of God.

Moses provides an example of a very common leadership approach—finding inspiration in a moment of solitude and then promoting that vision to a group of followers. According to several studies, nearly half of chief executives are introverts.[25] This doesn't necessarily equate to shyness, which is the common assumption. Introverts develop their insights and gather strength in solitude.[26] As a result, introverted executives tend to align closely with the Moses Model.

This model is not, however, restricted to introverts. I have seen many leaders—introverts and extroverts alike—employ the Moses Model in a similar pattern. A leader goes on vacation, reads a book, or takes a particularly hot shower one morning and—Boom!—has an inspired moment. Excitedly, the leader returns to the team proclaiming a new vision. Very rarely is this new vision received as a brilliant notion that rallies one and all. In the vast majority of cases, the new vision falls on deaf ears as team members exchange knowing glances since it isn't the first time they've heard such proclamations. The leader passionately attempts to convince the team of the merit of the idea, and since the boss is declaring his or her grand vision with personal force and conviction, constructive debate vanishes. To the leader, it seems as if agreement has been reached, but it's merely quiet acquiescence on the part of the team.

The Moses Model is often effectively used by entrepreneurs forming a new venture while trying to marshal financial support or captivate talent. However, once a team is in place, this model often fails and fails badly. Alleged support for the vision—imposed by our would-be Moses—only lasts until the first rough spot along the way to the goal. At the first substantive challenge, doubt overwhelms action. Debate about direction overwhelms collaboration. Worse yet, arguments about direction rarely appear when the leader is present, which means the leader isn't even aware that debate is underway and the plan is careening off track. Moses had help from God and still had trouble. If you follow this model, especially without divine intervention, you are likely to have trouble as well. Use it with caution!

The Trump Model

Donald Trump is feared, revered, and sometimes reviled but is always an exceptional and boisterous executive who likes to put on a good show. He serves as a wonderful archetype for this next model. While introverts seek regenerative solitude, extroverts draw their energy from groups. It's not that they don't need to be alone now and then. They just need the give and take of discussion to generate the synapses that help form their opinions and insights. They like to consider competing ideas in a public contest. This approach is not limited to extroverts, but they do tend to be the major users of it.

Leaders who employ this model operate from a sincere belief that competition in group interactions forms the best strategy, mission statement, project sequence, operating plan, annual objectives, or anything else an organization needs to choose from to be successful. Leaders who prefer the Trump Model also relish the drama that ensues while their underlings vie for a blessing on a project or business plan. The group discussion process often begins well enough but fails in the end because the competition is stacked.

In the Trump Model, parties compete for the leader's approval. But when Mr. Trump speaks, his lieutenants instantly adjust their world view—intentionally or subconsciously—to more closely align with his. This is a reasonable and rational reaction to try to win approval, but it creates an inherent bias. Instead of having the best idea win based on its merits, the idea or project that wins merely fits the explicit or deduced views of the leader. In effect, the Trump Model is merely a high drama version of dictating the outcome. The Trump Model isn't always invoked intentionally, but I have seen more than one leader deliberately use it as a club for beating people into submission in a pitched, public battle that is as one-sided as a contest between a gladiator and his heavily armed and defended emperor.

GLADIATOR VERSUS EMPEROR

Ralph led a large, multinational corporation and gathered his executive team weekly to discuss plans and status. In the midst of a discussion about a new project, Ralph would often assert his own view and then cajole his executives to propose alternate ideas on how to proceed. Ralph would then publicly impugn the intellect or character of any executive who had the audacity to present an idea not in alignment with his own stated view. At the first instance of the disagreement, Ralph would say, "Oh my, you are smarter than that. I'll give you time to reconsider." If the executive persisted into a second instance of disagreement, Ralph would say, "Are you a masochist?" If the hapless executive dared a third round of disagreement with Ralph, he'd launch into a tirade, visibly shaking with frustration and on a bad day would even hurl something against a wall.

Do you think this approach helped bring the team together around Ralph? Of course not. It did provide months of amusing retellings for those who had witnessed or triggered the antics. Inevitably these ego-bashing exercises resulted in the executive team dutifully complying with projects and objectives inferred from the debate. As you might expect, for nearly a decade, Ralph's team fell short of meeting almost every objective set in those brutally comic planning sessions.

Even if a leader is more rational or benign than Ralph in a group planning session and merely declares a strong opinion or suggestion, the creativity is still sucked out of the room. When Donald Trump speaks, his force of personality and his authority dramatically influences the room. And whether you find it an honor or an insult, every leader at least slightly resembles the public persona Mr. Trump has so carefully crafted. When you create a contest to declare a winner from among projects, priorities, or ideas, please remember they are watching everything you say and do for a hint of what you think is best.

THE SOCRATES MODEL

How do you avoid the pitfalls in the Moses and Trump models? Getting people with diverse personal and professional needs and wants to agree on a mission is not easy. For help, we turn to our next archetype, Socrates. He was a brilliant Greek philosopher immortalized by Plato's dialogues, and his approach to learning and views on ethics has influenced generations of scholars and leaders for well over two thousand years. Socrates pursued truth through debate, and his approach emphasized the use of challenging questions to pierce into topics to attain useful insights.

To lead using the Socrates Model, you must ask questions not only in group meetings, but also as a course of daily practice with the individuals in your organization. You must spend far more time listening than speaking. In group settings, this means calling intentionally on those who are silent to encourage them to express their views. When you do offer an opinion, you should play contrarian and offer opposing assertions deliberately to instigate debate and then harness the group's discussion to foster a respectful and rational contest among competing assertions.

FOSTERING RESPECTFUL DEBATE

Father Carl was in the midst of a significant remodel of his church, and the leadership group from the parish was discussing the proper placement of the main crucifix. This was a particularly sensitive topic on the verge of heated argument and as a result had been tabled many times before. Father Carl knew that if he insisted on a specific placement, several leaders in the community would complain bitterly for years about having their opinion disregarded, creating dissent he could ill afford since much of the capital for the remodel was donated by those very community leaders.

So he asserted a novel position based on a progressive interpretation of Vatican II—Father Carl proposed that rather than placing the crucifix on the far wall across from the entrance, they consider tucking the crucifix behind a vestibule so that it would provide a private space for reflection and prayer. Meanwhile the parish itself, in the pews surrounding the altar in the center of the hall, would serve as the focus during mass.

After a moment of dead silence, debate exploded. It roared for days, then weeks. Community leaders argued, interpreted church rules, and solicited the opinion of the church hierarchy. Father Carl calmly listened to each member of the leadership team and encouraged those who were more soft-spoken to express their views. The pastor urged prayer, reflection, and patient research into the best options that other parishes had considered. Above all, he expressed his openness to alternatives.

The ruse worked. After weeks of debate, the community leaders reached an agreement. Ironically, the community finally agreed that the best place for the crucifix in the newly remodeled church was slightly tucked behind one vestibule so that the parish and the altar would be the focus of the mass, but enough of the crucifix was visible to keep the more conservative parishioners happy.

This story illustrates a leader's key role in reaching consensus and also the impact a suggestion can have. You must seed the discussion to provoke the team to debate and then facilitate that discussion to uncover all the implicit assumptions, agendas, and opinions. In the process, you get the team to agree on something they would not have otherwise considered, and you persuade them to make a conscious agreement that they have had time to internalize and fully embrace. And sometimes you end up with a solution very close to what you had suggested in the first place, even if it was just to provoke a discussion.

What is the risk of using the Socrates Model? Endless swirl. A team sometimes needs even the most patient and Socratic leader to assert direction, especially if a clear decision doesn't emerge in the time available to choose. When using the Socrates Model, you must suspend opinion until the last reasonable moment. If the discussion hasn't led to an agreed-upon mission after the dissenters and creative thinkers have voiced their ideas and heard those of others, the team will naturally call on you to choose. At that point, you can impose your will and do so effectively. In a Socrates Model, the team is pulling you into a choice they can embrace, whereas in a Moses or Trump Model, you are explicitly or implicitly dictating a choice to the team.

CONVERTING ASSERTIONS INTO QUESTIONS

For most people, making assertions is a life habit ingrained from many years of education requiring rapid, correct responses and a bit of competitive drive. Now that you are a leader, you need to become skilled at asking questions if you want to avoid the hazards of the Trump and Moses Models. A good way to practice the Socratic Model is to keep track of all the assertions you make during the next week. You can do it yourself, or you can ask someone on your team to help you keep track of them. Either way, you need to develop a list of typical assertions you make. To further benefit from this exercise, review it and convert each assertion into a question. Here are some examples to help you get started:

Assertion	Converted to Question
I don't believe this trend will continue.	What assumptions are you making?
A reduction doesn't make sense to me.	How did you come to that conclusion?
I am fairly certain it can be done.	What is stopping you from doing that?
I am sure of it.	What do you see?
I agree completely.	What happens if we are wrong?
I want this done by Monday.	What do you need to get this done by Monday?
I need it sooner.	What do you need to progress faster?
We can't afford that.	Is there a way to proceed without that?

If you find yourself unsure of what to ask, remember that the most powerful tool you have as a leader is the question, "Why not?" You can apply this quite easily. Every assertion you generate is a response to either an event or another person's assertion. Rather than stating your opinion, practice inverting your observation into its opposite, and then ask why it isn't so. In the first example above, you can replace "I don't believe this trend will continue" with "Why wouldn't this trend come to an end?" A similar inversion can be crafted for each example. I am not suggesting you become a Socratic automaton. I am urging you to balance your interactions with your team by asking more questions. Besides, asking questions is an easy exercise with very little risk. In particular, when you frequently ask, "Why not?" even if it is a stretch, you will find that you are pushing your team toward excellence. Asking questions creates an engaging relationship and allows your team to demonstrate through facts

> If you find yourself unsure of what to ask, remember that the most powerful tool you have as a leader is the question, "Why not?"

and logic what can and cannot be done—automatically surfacing any implicit, faulty assumptions in the process.

CUTTING TO THE CHASE

We have now explored several approaches to reaching consensus as a team. It is important to note that even if all say they agree, there will always be at least one straggler in the group who isn't actually on board. That person might not voice it, but you can be certain he or she is still quite uncomfortable with the agreed-upon mission. In the process of reaching consensus, if you have cut off the conversation for the sake of saving time or out of a judgment that enough debate has taken place, remember that the conversation continues after you shut it off—just not while you're present. People who weren't heard in an open forum will find a private outlet to vent their spleen, usually to the detriment of your organization.

You must flush out those stragglers. This requires you to listen very carefully with all your senses, and it requires you to trust your instincts. If you have a hunch some aren't quite on board, do not hesitate. Approach them in private and give them room to voice a contrarian position. It's all right if they voice doubts privately with you or in a leadership team setting. That is the best place to explore concerns, issues, and doubts they still harbor. It is not acceptable, however, if someone advocates a contrary position directly to his or her own staff or, worse yet, to people outside the organization. This is tantamount to sabotage, and even a small incident can end up being a significant problem.

Scott McNeely, the highly respected CEO of computer maker Sun Microsystems, used a swift blade to cut through a half-committed challenger hiding in his team. Once a plan of record was in place, he demanded, "Agree and commit, or disagree and commit, or get the hell out of the way."[27] Mr. McNeely's approach effectively enforces alignment when stragglers start promoting their own agendas, but you have to reserve the tactic until after a reasonable discussion to consider alternative approaches and plans. Otherwise, you are just back to using the Trump Model as a bashing instrument for your will.

CONSENSUS BECOMES CONVICTION

In a severely time-constrained situation with very high stakes, demanding that your team simply take orders is your most efficient means of aligning them toward an objective. This is, however, a rare moment for most leaders of organizations. In the vast majority of situations, you have time to consider alternatives. Your job as the leader is to motivate and inspire your team to exert sustained effort toward a goal, typically over a period of weeks, months, or years. Your team needs to feel firm conviction in the mission in order to face with courage the seemingly insurmountable challenges that are always encountered along the way to achieving any mission worthy of pursuit. Engaging them in an open exchange of ideas converts consensus into conviction and provides the best way to create the relationship that allows you to achieve the goals you have set forth.

> ## QUICK CUES—REACHING CONSENSUS
>
> Establish a timeline for reaching consensus.
>
> Consciously choose a model: Moses, Trump, or Socrates.
>
> Suspend your opinions.
>
> Ask questions and frequently ask, "Why not?"
>
> Play contrarian whenever you can. Propose the opposite to provoke debate.
>
> When you decide it's time to agree, demand commitment.

CHAPTER 10

MAKING TOUGH CHOICES

The only wisdom is in knowing you know nothing.

Socrates[28]

I once observed a CEO while he personally supervised his executive suite remodel and—no joke—queried his top leaders for days on color choices, wood choices, and whether the bathroom fixtures should have satin nickel or brushed nickel finish. Please, if you do nothing else as a result of reading this book, ensure you focus your precious time and opportunity for leadership on something more worthy than office remodeling.

The bathroom hardware debate may seem like an example of exaggerated attention to detail, but when put into context, this situation illustrates how fear of failure can drive behavior. The CEO's company was bleeding profit losses from a bloated organization structure and operational inefficiency, yet he chose to avoid considering staff and expense reduction proposals to solve the cash flow dilemma. He simultaneously deferred discussion on product improvements and pricing changes while competitors picked off key accounts month after month, using clever pricing schemes and promoting new features. His business languished as a host of unaddressed challenges waited for his decisions, yet he focused intently on the bathroom design. Why? It gave him a sense of control over outcome. Choosing satin nickel fixtures was less risky and easier to define than which employees to layoff. Choosing cherry wood cabinets was far easier to specify than which product features might outmaneuver the competition.

Cultivate Courage

You need to invest your most precious asset—your time—on issues that matter most to the people you are affecting with your decisions. Remember, even a leader with only three employees will impact thousands of people over time. And while you may feel a sense of satisfaction by insisting on color schemes, furniture placement, or other aspects over which you have authority and some control, you owe it to yourself and your organization to spend your time and attention on the most challenging decisions that your team faces.

Abraham Lincoln once said, "Courage is not the absence of fear. It is going forward in the face of it." Great leaders distinguish themselves by demonstrating an ability to choose a path and follow it in a situation where others are paralyzed by fear of failure. You may never be tested with leading a nation through civil war, but you will at times need to choose from undesirable or obscure paths. Furthermore, every leader must make decisions based on imperfect data. In fact, the more imperfect the data, the more likely you will be the one deciding. If there is sufficient data, rest assured your team will be making the decision or, at the very least, asserting specific recommendations. And if perfect information for making decisions was readily available, we could write an algorithm and have a computer make decisions for you.

No, you don't get the easy decisions. By definition, you are the leader so you have to make tough choices. Facing the hardest choices will have an emotional impact on you and, therefore, those around you. We suffer a little trauma every time a significant decision is made. And with each difficult decision, you will have to overcome doubt that can manifest either as a fear of failure or as a source of possibility. The difference is in whether you reject or embrace doubt.

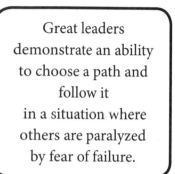

Great leaders demonstrate an ability to choose a path and follow it in a situation where others are paralyzed by fear of failure.

It's like being a fire chief at a massive, multi-story blaze. The heat is breathtaking. You have been training for years how to get your team into a burning building, find the survivors, and bring them all—rescued and rescuers—to safety. Now you stand before that fire with dry mouth and heavy innards not knowing if you will live or die, not knowing where the stranded victims are in the building, not knowing where the safest path lies, and not willing to walk away and head for the safety of home. You must choose and you must act. You must also send others from your team into that blaze, facing the same unknowns. And you must do it quickly—the fire is raging and taking its toll on the structure. There is no time to waste.

Most of us will never face a blazing fire, but time and again I see normally bold men and women gaze with tremendous uncertainty as they suffer indecision about how much to invest in a product line, whether to expand an operation, how to choose from strategy alternatives, whether to reduce expenses, and how to choose from seemingly equal candidates for a key position. The list goes on and on. Our minds produce the same kind of stress for our bodies whether we are faced with a burning building, a layoff, a sudden spike in demand, or a major investment. Making tough choices requires courage, which has three main components: doubt, choice, and action.

Doubt. As a leader, you must learn to revel in doubt. When others become uncomfortable with the lack of solid information or clear choices, you must be at ease. When the moment comes to make a decision that has significant impact on your organization, it is natural to feel a sense of doubt. Our ego forms an impulse to make the "right" choice that will prove we are the right person for the job and, therefore, deserve the role of leader. The instant that impulse appears in our mind, fear is born. Doubt about the outcome of your decision merges with the desire to be right, and fear of failure appears.

Whenever you sense a bit of apprehension about a decision, you can be certain it is fear of failure. Don't avoid it. Take a deep breath and examine that apprehension to discover for yourself where it originates. That is the first step to overcoming fear. For some leaders, that sense of fear is motivating. It can drive the ego into high gear. Chest-thumping, bold claims about winning, crushing the competition, and other forms of braggadocio manifest. Consider the case of Bob:

> Doubt can manifest either as a fear of failure or as a source of possibility. The difference is in whether you reject or embrace doubt.

SHOUTING INTO THE CHASM

Bob was the head of sales for a successful manufacturer, and his team had just barely made quota for the first half of the year. Once they had finished evaluating their prospects for the second half of the year, it was clear they had little chance of hitting their financial targets for the rest of the year. Only after he demanded that a second evaluation be performed did he believe the dilemma. He brought his key sales leaders together for an expensive meal complete with ample fine wine. During the dinner he stood up and said in his characteristically vigorous voice, "We have had a great first half and are here to celebrate. We are the best in the world at this game. The plan we signed up for in the second half is tall, but it's achievable if we say it is. We will not lose any deals these next six months. Damn it! It isn't good enough to win. Everybody else must lose. Are you with me? Let's kick some ass!" The team, well lubricated with food and wine, erupted in enthusiastic applause and a few "Hell yeahs!" to boot.

They worked hard for the next six months but despite their efforts did not succeed in making quota. They missed their annual goals by 7 percent, causing each team member to lose a substantial portion of their bonus compensation. Although they should have felt great pride in what they did accomplish and what they learned as they attempted to win at such odds, instead they felt miserable for having fought and missed the mark. Several of the best sales executives in that team left the following year because they felt set up for failure.

Shouting into the chasm of doubt can motivate and inspire a team. But this approach wears thin quickly and worse yet, as it did with Bob, can backfire if the outcome doesn't match the claims made during the rallying.

FACING YOUR FEAR

You must be willing to embrace doubt deliberately. That means when that nagging sense of doubt appears, take a deep breath, just as you have practiced during the listening exercise earlier in this book. Settle into that doubt and listen to it. When you face doubt squarely rather than avoiding it or shouting at it, you will see very clearly that doubt is the source of possibility, creativity, and hope. Doubt appears because we don't know the future or the outcome of our challenging decisions. This means, of course, that the future holds the possibility of not only failure but also success. Even more exciting, the future inevitability presents a new opportunity as a result of any choice we make today, an option inconceivable now because we are still consumed with an unresolved, challenging decision at this moment.

Embracing doubt requires one more step—suspending judgment. For a moment, take in all the facts and options at your disposal, breathe slowly, and listen carefully. If you then react with Shakespearean rowdiness along the lines of, "Once more unto the breach, dear friends, once more," then have at it and have fun. Win or lose in a blaze of glory if you like. If, on the other hand, you react with a sense of foreboding, you should interpret that unease as evidence that your ego

> Doubt is not your enemy; it is your source of greatness.

is eager to get it right. Thank your ego for the warning, tell it to sit down, and remind yourself that doubt is the source of possibility. I promise that if you practice the listening exercise every day, then you will face even the most stomach-churning doubt more calmly after one deep breath. If you listen to your doubt directly and suspend judgment, you will see directly into creativity and possibility. You are a leader. The only certainty is uncertainty, so suck it up and get used to it. Doubt is not your enemy; it is your source of greatness.

Choice. Only after learning to relax into doubt does the fear of failure grow still in our hearts. When you grow accustomed to doubt, it is gradually and naturally replaced with an urge to choose. As a leader, it is your right and obligation to take a firm stance in the face of uncertainty. You must exercise your responsibility to choose in spite of doubts about the facts, doubts about abilities, doubts about staff and partners, and more doubts than can ever be listed here.

If you doubt deeply enough, you will doubt even doubt itself which leads to freedom. Since you cannot know for certain anything that lies in the future, you are truly free to choose. You choose and the outcome you hope for either emerges or doesn't. Either way, you will face new choices and have the opportunity to choose again. This makes even the most difficult decision a bit less critical. If you must be 100 percent certain of the outcome, then of course your choice matters. But you cannot be 100 percent certain when making the tough choices. They are by definition ambiguous and uncertain. In fact, what you choose is not nearly as important as how you choose because your relationships are formed and cultivated through your actions more than on the milestones you achieve.

CHECKLIST FOR CHOOSING

Before finalizing your next choice, ask yourself:

- ❑ Have you considered all the facts and options available to you in the time you have?

- ❑ Have you solicited your most trusted advisors?

- ❑ Have you openly shared your doubts with your most valuable staff members?

- ❑ Have you listened carefully?

- ❑ Are you procrastinating or being thoughtful?

- ❑ Are you being impetuous or responding to material urgency?

- ❑ Have you ensured that your prime objective is the well-being of your team, your sponsors, your partners or customers, and your community?

If you have done all this, it is time to choose. The source of boldness that breaks the stalemate of analysis is accepting that you cannot know and yet here and now the decision falls to you. In this moment, whether it is a belief in fate, destiny, the will of God, or a fervent hope in your ability to choose well, you choose because you must. As a leader in this moment, you choose because you have the right and obligation to choose. Not choosing is abdication.

I have seen many brilliant leaders flounder in moments of choice. They hesitate not from of a lack of courage, but from an obsession with achieving the optimum outcome. They know it is impossible to choose with certainty, so they buy time to see if they can better predict the best path. They try to keep all the choices viable until some mythical moment arrives when it is best to decide—in a word, they hedge.

CHOOSING EVERYTHING IS CHOOSING NOTHING

Julia had been running her company for about ten years. She was a clever entrepreneur who led vibrant growth even while the market around her imploded. It was clear, however, that her company had reached a plateau. Sales growth had tapered off and new competitors had started to erode her market dominance. To grow again, Julia needed to lead her company into uncharted waters. The options her team faced included:

1. Stick with the current product and ride it out, managing for profitability rather than revenue growth.

2. Use part of current profits to launch a new set of features that make current products better than the competition's.

3. Combine cash reserves and current profits to acquire new assets and then launch into a promising new product line altogether.

Julia chose all three and sincerely believed she had made a choice. She instructed one of her executives to lead a profitability initiative, including cutting staff and expenses to improve profit growth. She assigned another executive the responsibility of enhancing the current product line and insisted to the bewildered executive that it was possible even though staff and expenses had been reduced. Julia assigned yet another executive the task of soliciting target acquisitions and building a business plan to launch an entirely new business line. The company floundered for two years with little growth in sales or profit and no substantive change in products. About 60 percent of the executives left the company. And employee morale was abysmal.

CHOICE CREATES POSSIBILITIES

Julia had failed to make a tough choice in hopes of avoiding the wrong choice. Although it is true that any choice eliminates possibilities, it is also true that each choice creates new opportunities. Let's reconsider Julia's situation to explore how constraining yourself to one choice can unleash new choices. Here are some positive outcomes that might have happened had Julia been brave enough to make a choice and stick to it:

Alternatives	Result of Focus
Stick with the current product and optimize for profitability.	They might have become a very desirable target for a larger company looking for a market leader that added profitability.
Invest some of the current profits into feature enhancements on the current product.	They likely would have hired new employees who might have conceived new features, competitive positions, or operating efficiencies.

Alternatives	Result of Focus
Invest out of a flat business by using all the available cash and profits of the company.	They might have completed the same kind of radical and lucrative transformation that Scott Paper accomplished decades ago as it transformed from a low margin commodity supplier to a higher margin consumer goods company.[29]

Yes, it is true each of these could have led to suboptimal results. But you cannot have perfect information about the future outcome of your alternatives. Hesitating to choose in order to obtain more information or hedge your choices is usually an exercise in futility, especially for the more ambiguous and higher stakes choices. There is never enough information to be 100 percent sure, and in just a short time, new variables and situations emerge that only add to the complexity and difficulty of the decisions you must make. In many cases, waiting to choose will cost you the choice and in some cases waiting will cost you the endeavor.

Action. The last component of making the tough choice is decisive action. There is no leadership without action. Of course, there is also a dilemma inherent in this. Leadership is not a soloist occupation—it is a relationship with other people. It isn't only

> You have the right and obligation to choose.
> Not choosing is abdication.

your action that is required. You must get other people to act. Fortunately, human beings are social creatures that move in response to the leader and the group's momentum. If you take action, then those whom you lead are very likely to cascade into action as well.

In leadership, action without doubt is hubris, and doubt without action is paralysis. For most people, the latter half of this axiom is the rub. I have worked closely with many confident, successful leaders who suffered in private with action paralysis. Even after thorough and insightful evaluation and firm decision making, they do not act. A week will go by after their action deadline has passed, and when we meet again, their first reaction is a sheepish grin and a shrugged confession of "No, I haven't done that yet. I don't know what the heck is stopping me."

> Action without
> doubt is hubris.
> Doubt without action
> is paralysis.

What is stopping them? Very simply—a lack of practice. After sifting fact from fiction and taking a position despite lack of sufficient evidence to know fully the best course of action, you must act with confidence as though you know for sure. Stop thinking about it. Don't hedge. Take a deep breath, declare a course, and exhort others to join. Then observe what choices appear as a result of your actions. I guarantee new choices will appear almost immediately, so pay attention. Opportunity is moments away.

START SIMPLE

Most firefighters, emergency medical technicians, police, and military field commanders I have met are well trained through drills in which they must take action in moments of great stress. They repeat the same activities over and over until they become second nature—a reflex. Similarly, actors, athletes, musicians, and other performing artists use repetition and rehearsal so that when the pressure to perform is on, there is no need to think or hesitate—they just do it.

If you struggle in your leadership role to take action even after thoughtful consideration and making a firm choice, know that this hesitation comes with the territory. Every leader struggles with this because the choices typically don't repeat. Each situation is usually different. To overcome any halting procrastination, you need to practice decisiveness. You could get firefighter or acting training, or you could start training in a team sport and then practice with high-action professionals. For most of us who are not pursuing those career choices, it isn't practical. Even if it were possible, it wouldn't help very much because it isn't your regular vocational environment. Instead, you can start with the easy choices at work. What matters is consciously practicing the *Doubt—Choice—Action* pattern in a deliberate and methodical way, even with the mundane choices.

Here is a simple illustration. Go to a restaurant you have not visited before and consider the tiny doubt you feel when choosing from among the menu selections. Don't ask questions. Force the doubt. You don't know which entrée is best. You don't know the chef or the quality of the produce and meat acquired that morning. You don't know if the restaurant has the skilled staff to prepare the entrees well. Choose anyway, and if you hesitate, push yourself to act quickly through that choice, and tell the waiter what you want. Know that if you deeply regret that choice, you can call the waiter back, but then again, that is a new choice to make. Know that if the food arrives and isn't to your liking, you can always send it back, but then again, that is a new choice to make. Even in this mundane example in which you artificially created doubt and forced yourself to choose, you created new choices.

Every day you face choices this simple at work. When will you meet? What is the objective? How many people do you need? What skills are required for the project? The list is endless. Practice the deliberate and conscious mental pattern of *Doubt—Choice—Action* in every situation, and soon choosing and action will go hand-in-hand and become second nature. A reflex action. Your mind and body will have developed a kind of muscle memory that almost forces you to act, even during the tough times you will face as a leader. You are a leader, so take advantage of every opportunity you have to practice *Doubt— Choice—Action* so that you master it. Your team needs you to be good at this, so please don't avoid the exercise.

To close, this chapter, I'd like to share one of my favorite examples of a leader making a tough choice. You are not the first to face this harsh function in leadership, and you will not be the last. Witness the moment when Julius Caesar stood at the Rubicon:

Alea Iacta Est

In 49 BCE, the Roman republic was corrupt to the core. The vast majority of citizens and peasants at this time in history barely eked out a living while a small group of aristocrats and their favored friends lived in lavish homes with food and wine to spare. The republic was almost constantly under barbarian assault. Julius Caesar had command of an army in northern Italy, and the narrow Rubicon River was the boundary between his assigned province and Rome. He had come to the river with one of his legions of troops because of a series of political and military events that had brought Caesar and his rival Pompey to a showdown for control of the republic.

Under Pompey's influence, the Senate called for Caesar to relinquish his command, which would end his political career. If Caesar failed to obey, he would be hunted down and killed. If he agreed to step down from his post, his rival would rule and then likely prosecute and kill him anyway. And so Caesar marched on Rome, but as he approached the Rubicon, he fell silent and waited at the water's edge. His men grew impatient and wondered. Were they going to fight for glory or death, or would they now return on a long march back in resignation? Sweat grew on his brow. His heart pounded and his arms grew heavy. If he crossed the Rubicon, there would be civil war. Thousands would perish and the republic would teeter on the brink of destruction. If he retreated, Pompey would most certainly hunt him down, and the republic would likely be destroyed.

After a period of staring silently at the river, muttering to himself, and taking counsel from his closest and most loyal men, Caesar finally took a deep breath and declared, "*Alea Iacta Est* [the die is cast]." Caesar faced great doubt about the future. The outcome was no more certain than his spoken roll of the die. He could only be certain that his intention was for the betterment of the world in which he lived. He crossed the river with his men, fought a bloody civil war for control of the republic, won, and launched a military and economic expansion that built an empire which lasted another four hundred years and influenced much of Western civilization—in art, religion, literature, law, and social structure—and still has influence today, two thousand years later.[30]

You might not be leading an army into a bloody, civil war. But each time you face a difficult choice in your organization's life cycle, you stand with Caesar. When you stand at your Rubicon, learn from him. Yes, it can be daunting to make a difficult choice. Yes, it is reasonable to have great doubt. Do your homework. Learn everything you can in the time you have; consider all your options in the time you have. Then breathe deeply and slowly, bravely explore that doubt, and make certain that your choice and your actions are for a better future for the vast majority of those whom you affect with your decision. Then put everything away, stop thinking, and act—*Alea Iacta Est.*

QUICK CUES—MAKING TOUGH CHOICES

Doubt is your friend so listen carefully—face your fear of failure.

Do your homework then choose, don't hedge.

Choosing despite uncertainty is your right and obligation.

Choose a path that benefits the majority of those whom you affect with your actions.

After you choose, stop thinking and act.

There is no leadership without action.

CHAPTER 11

HARNESSING AMBITION

Nature is complete because it does not serve itself.
The sage places himself after and finds himself before,
ignores his desire and finds himself content.
He is complete because he does not serve himself.

Lao Tzu[31]

Ambition is a word often used as a pejorative. Merriam-Webster declares the primary definition as an ardent desire for rank, fame, or power. That seems too simplistic to me. Words such as optimism, aspiration, faith, or visionary might help soften this notion, but for a discussion about leadership, they don't hit the mark nearly as well as the visceral and candid *ambition*. In truth, can you think of one great leader who did not have ambition? Leadership without ambition is a meat puppet, an empty suit, an unappealing bag of mostly water. In my view, ambition is neither vile nor honorable. It is an elemental, human quality. The real question is—where is your ambition pointed?

You have ambition—I am certain of that. You picked up this book and started reading it, in part, because you have a desire to lead well. You might have hoped to find a nugget of wisdom, a suggestion, or a hint to improve your chances of success. To lead, you must have ambition. To lead well, you must have great ambition. You must act boldly, and you must be willing to pay the price. You must be willing to surrender your personal wants to the needs of those you lead. It is that particular act of sacrifice, often born of ambition, which brings about leadership excellence.

It's Not about You

There are many successful leaders who began their careers yearning for success, fame, power, or wealth. This is quite typical among young men and women, and it is the same in every country and in every language I have ever encountered. There is nothing unusual about this motivation as a starting point, but as I've already asserted, our decisions and actions as leaders are intertwined with the lives of those we lead and also those with whom they live and work. Leadership is an intricate web of relationships. Build them and you succeed. Break them and you fail. Base them on something meaningful and magnificent, and you help build a better world. This is true even if it's just a better youth soccer team filled with motivated, inspired kids. If this is true for a youth soccer coach, then how much more so for a police chief, school principal, CEO, or a pastor? Every leadership role has the opportunity to contribute significantly to this world. Do not underestimate the impact you have, no matter how provincial the setting or how seemingly insignificant the mission. Lead well and you build a better community. It's as simple as that.

> You must be willing to surrender your personal wants to the needs of those you lead.

Put aside your ego for a moment and consider a wider view of why you are in a leadership role in the first place. If you have already mastered some of the elements in this book, you probably have had leadership thrust upon you. If you do in fact ardently desire rank, power, and fame, then remember you are in a leadership role because it suits the people you lead. It suits some better than others, but either way, it serves their own self-interests to have you lead at this moment. Whether you are the selfless master or selfish novice, you didn't get a leadership role because you are special. You got this role because the people you lead need you there now.

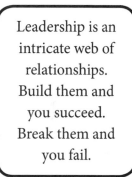

Leadership is an intricate web of relationships. Build them and you succeed. Break them and you fail.

Perhaps, they need a place to perfect their skills. Or, they don't want to invest effort into leading the team. They don't have the confidence to lead. They believe in the mission. They want a paycheck. They want to belong. They want someone else to organize. They need someone to grow or protect their investment. They like the people in the organization. Regardless of the specific motivations of the people you lead, your leadership role is not about you. It never was. It's about them.

If you are sincere and thoughtful about your leadership role, then you are already investing the majority of your waking—and some sleeping—hours in leading your organization. Why are you doing this? Is it for your fame? Your wealth? Your personal satisfaction? Your professional development? Only that? Why not aspire for something more? Are you afraid to take it on? Are you unwilling to make the effort? Please note, the higher the aspiration and the more inclusive the benefit of your ambition, the more you create a sustainable and successful effort that outlasts your own personal investment of time and energy. Anything less is a waste of your opportunity, and if you insist on serving your own self-interests, it will almost assuredly lead to disaster. Not convinced?

CORPORATE CHIEFS

What is the difference between Kenneth Lay and Bill Gates? Both wielded power, fame, and had high rank. Both created companies that generated many billions of dollars in shareholder wealth and tens of thousands of jobs. An idealistic, youthful Gates instituted an egalitarian equity structure that severely diluted his own stake and made over ten thousand employees millionaires.[32] An experienced, industrious Lay allowed his executives to mislead employees and investors while pocketing millions for themselves. Software mogul Gates is now spending the bulk of his time on philanthropic endeavors, while the veteran energy industry chief executive Lay was vilified, indicted, convicted of securities fraud, and died of misery and heart failure.[33]

REVEREND SHEPHERDS

Consider Desmond Tutu and Jim Bakker. Each has wielded power, fame, and immense popularity as the leader of a church. Both men have moved millions of the faithful to generously devote time and money to advance their cause. Desmond Tutu, the Anglican cleric who played a prominent role in ending apartheid in South Africa, used his leadership platform to raise money and press for civil rights, AIDS education and prevention, and compassion. He was awarded the Nobel Peace Prize in 1984.[34] The charismatic and fiery Jim Bakker, who with his wife Tammy Faye Bakker helped create the popular *700 Club* flagship television program of the Christian Broadcast Network, preached judgment and invective against those who did not follow his biblical interpretation. He succumbed to sexual and financial scandal, was subsequently arrested, imprisoned for fraud, and divorced.[35]

NATION BUILDERS

Compare Adolf Hitler and Mahatma Gandhi. Each had rank, fame, and power and the ambition to build a nation. For ten years, Hitler promoted socialism and anti-Semitism and advocated a bold military expansion in the name of rebuilding a Germany that had been left ravaged after the First World War.[36] For more than twenty years, Gandhi promoted non-violence, non-cooperation, and peaceful resistance to frustrate British control and create leverage in negotiating a successful secession.[37] Under Hitler, Germany was diminished even further than when he had started, and although the country has economically recovered, it still suffers his shame and dishonor fifty years after his death. Gandhi's India successfully established its independence and, in the past half century, has risen to become one of the most educated, industrious, and successful nations on earth.

These comparisons are not meant to impugn one or laud the other but serve as object lessons for every leader. Bold choices are not enough. A series of victories are not enough. It's only when you choose an ambition that creates benefit for many, even if it means less for you now, that you create a legacy of excellence. Focus on your own wants and you will destroy more than you create. Leadership is an amplifier of your ambition. Be careful where you point it!

It's worth repeating this verbatim. The greater the aspiration and the more inclusive the benefit of your ambition, the more you create a sustainable and successful effort that outlasts your own personal investment of time and energy. Anything less is a waste of your opportunity, and if you insist on serving your own self-interests, it will almost assuredly lead to disaster. As you lead, will you seek executive privilege or egalitarian equity? Will you pursue equal rights or personal peccadilloes? Will you advocate fighting for domination or negotiating for parity? It's up to you—choose wisely.

HOPE IS YOUR ENGINE

As the leader, you have the privilege of articulating the ambition of your organization. If you wish to inspire, you must focus your organization on hope. Hope is the locomotive that pulls your ambition across time, space, boredom, and dilemma. It is an engine that outlasts your goals, objectives, and daily effort. There are many historical and contemporary examples of leaders who have used fear as a source of motivation. Fear is a motivator but is also an instrument used to promote division or preservation. Divisiveness, exclusivity, and protectionism rarely lead to lasting value and almost always lead to suffering.

If you choose to harness your ambition around hope, know that your resolve for hope over fear will be tested. All leaders must stand their ground under fire, at times under active and aggressive persecution. What matters most is not what you promise in the early days—it's what you do when those hopes are tested. And you will be tested, so what will you do? Great leaders face daunting challenges with resolve, make bold

> An ambition harnessed around hope provides everyone you lead with the force of will to continue when the odds mount heavily against you.

choices, act selflessly, and thereby inspire others for a better future. An ambition harnessed around hope provides everyone you lead with the necessary force of will to continue even when the odds mount heavily against you. Hope creates the possibility of disappointment, but it also makes the effort and sacrifice worthwhile. If leadership is a relationship in which one person inspires and motivates a group into action toward a common goal, then your most critical function as a leader is to make that goal worthy of all the effort. Your ambition must be bold and at least a little impudent or it isn't bold enough.

This is not just for momentous historical choices and world leaders of nations. It's true for principals and preachers, chief surgeons and teachers, coaches and lawyers, project managers and executives, police chiefs and pastry chefs. Do you really think Dr. Robert Jarvik didn't have naysayers all around him when he began his quest to create the artificial heart? When Joseph B. Strauss proposed a design for the Golden Gate Bridge, he was considered a hopeless dreamer by most. Wolfgang Puck is one of the best-known chefs and food industry tycoons in the world yet began his career learning cooking from his mother and toiling in the kitchen for years as an apprentice. Every leader has enormous influence, no matter where he or she starts. Every leader with an ambition harnessed around hope contributes significantly to the world we share. No industry, discipline, or field of endeavor is too small. If you challenge people to strive toward a bold future worthy of their efforts, they will respond with inventiveness, effort and determination for years. And in the process, you help make this a better world.

Get On with It

Hopefully you are now more aware than ever of the impact you have on the people in your organization, your community, and the world at large. This book has shared some insights into specific behaviors you can practice each day to hone and perfect your leadership. With practice, you can master each of the fundamental skills of listening, storytelling, negotiating, and assessing people. Aspire to be a great leader because you can and your influence matters. Make the effort to become expert in assembling talent, reaching consensus, and making tough choices. Remember that when you put all these building blocks under a wide roof of ambition harnessed around hope, you have a structure that inspires well beyond the effort you make today.

Lastly, always bear in mind that leadership is an intricate web of relationships. You cannot succeed without those relationships—cultivate and cherish them and shield them well. If you are already in a leadership position, you have been given a rare gift in this life. Please do not squander it. Don't settle for a comfortable objective that serves only a few. Know that it is your right and obligation to be bold, provocative, and never boring. Be demanding and passionate, and above all, harness your ambition and point it toward a future that benefits all those whom you influence through your efforts.

Lead on!

QUICK CUES—HARNESSING AMBITION

It's not about you—it's about those you lead.

Aim for the unachievable and demand inclusivity.

Harness your ambition around hope.

Be bold, be provocative, never boring.

APPENDICES

Hiring a Coach

Sample Assessment Rubric

Notes & Sources

HIRING A COACH

Do you need a coach? No. Can a good coach help you? Yes. Most great leaders have done fine without a coach. Yet, it seems silly to steer an oil tanker up the Mississippi River without a local pilot, especially if one is available. It seems ridiculous to climb Mount Everest without a Sherpa, especially if one is available. It might be romantic to go it alone, but you aren't in a leadership role for yourself. You will impact thousands of people, so be smart. Use whatever resources you have to be a great leader. Read books and essays, study other leaders, and if you can find a good coach, hire one.

If you do hire a coach, be sure to seek one that acts like a coach by holding you accountable to your ambition while motivating and urging you toward excellence. Some coaches behave like pigeons that fly in, gently coo and get in the way.[38] Some coaches act like a mirror and merely reflect what you say or do, without pushing you to improve. A good coach listens carefully but also challenges your logic, motives, and actions. A good coach harnesses his or her own skills and experiences to encourage you and help you to sharpen yours. A good coach is a confidante that serves as a consistent observer and motivator to accelerate your development as a leader.

Hiring a highly qualified coach that can serve as a confidante can be quite useful. But remember: *caveat emptor*—there are more charlatans than qualified coaches in the marketplace. If you choose to hire a coach, do your homework and interview candidates meticulously—review their training and references but pay close attention to their experience in leadership. You don't want someone simply following one of the popular coaching templates. You want someone who can combine rigorous coaching methodology with insights based on personal leadership experience.

WHEN TO HIRE A COACH

First and foremost, to receive effective coaching you need to be open to learning new ideas, strategies, and skills and be ready to put it all into practice. Unless you are ready to make the effort, don't waste your time or money on a coach. Also, leaders rarely hire a coach while everything is going well. Usually, there is a trigger event that causes you to look for help. Some of the more common drivers are:

❑   Your organization is underachieving. You have tried bullying, pleading, workshops, or consultants, and you still aren't happy with results.

❑   Your board or team is dysfunctional, and you need a safe place to vent, evaluate, and explore options to improve performance.

❑   You recently accepted a leadership role and need a private place to explore openly your ideas, concerns, or weaknesses with a trusted, experienced confidante.

❑   You have been leading for years and are ready to transition out of your leadership role.

How Does Coaching Work?

Have you ever been coached for sports or performing arts? Did you connect well with your coach? Did he or she have a track record of leading teams or individuals to success? If you can answer yes to these questions, think back on those coaches and then ask yourself, "What did they do for me?" Now ask yourself, "What exactly is Michael Phelps' coach doing for Michael? What is Serena Williams' coach doing for Serena?"

Elite level coaching eliminates barriers and brings out your best. A good coach will observe and learn all about you and your skills, your style, and your talents. A good coach will use insights from that meticulous attention to help you clearly and honestly evaluate your strengths and areas for development. A good coach will motivate you to build confidence, technique, and unleash your talents so you can reach your greatest potential.

Research in the business arena indicates that coaching provides an excellent financial return on investment. Productivity studies have shown for decades that the simple act of setting goals yields measurable improvements in results. Since coached executives receive tools and develop skills that go far beyond simple goal setting, a greater improvement among coached executives would be expected. Research in this area is still nascent, but recent studies consistently show well over 500 percent return on investment in coaching.[39]

How Do You Pick a Coach?

Referrals from trusted friends or professional networks such as www.linkedin.com are great ways to find a coach. You can also visit the Web site of a professional coaching organization such as the International Coach Federation or Worldwide Association of Business Coaches to get a referral. Regardless of where you find one, you should spend a few sessions with the coach before settling on one. He or she should be willing to meet with you a few times on an exploratory basis. If your potential coach is any good, he or she will want to evaluate your situation, skills, openness, and sincerity before signing up with you.

SAMPLE ASSESSMENT RUBRIC

Very often it is harder to create from scratch than to react to an example. Here is a rubric that can serve as an example of how to define each standard of excellence you set. If you like something in this rubric sample, feel free to use it. If you don't like it, then react by adding, deleting, or editing it to fit your own experience and standards. Remember to keep it simple. You will not use this daily or even weekly if it's cumbersome and overly detailed. Just hit the main points in each element so you can commit them to memory.

It is far more effective to create this rubric with input from your peers and your team than by yourself. Your peers will validate your ideas and offer better ones. Reviewing with your team allows them to co-author how they are being evaluated, which gives them a sense of ownership in the process, and allows them to provide you with useful insights into what matters and what doesn't for your organization.

Also, collaborating with your team in the creation of this rubric educates and informs your team of your standards, which is more efficient and effective than crafting and selling a rubric on your own. In any case, have fun with this, keep it brief, and make it yours.

Workmanship
- ☐ Takes pride in superior results, work-product, and deliverables

- ☐ Is expedient and prompt

- ☐ Applies focused effort and meticulous attention to detail

Curiosity
- ☐ Has a strong, sincere desire to know and understand

- ☐ Eagerly probes for detail on history, logic, purpose, and value

- ☐ Remains unsatisfied with status quo; searches for alternatives

- ☐ Frequently expresses joy at learning something new

Willingness to admit error
- ☐ Declares obstacles in a timely fashion

- ☐ Shields staff from own errors in judgment

- ☐ Openly declares fault in order to advance conversation about solutions

Technical proficiency
- ❑ Strong aptitude, skill level, and experience in their field

- ❑ Demonstrated history of results and ability to explain in detail how achieved

- ❑ Well read in their field

- ❑ Best specific examples in each field or function that reports to you (list names of one or two people you consider exceptional in each line)

  - ❑ Field/Function #1: (e.g., Finance)

  - ❑ Field/Function #2: (e.g., Engineering)

  - ❑ Field/Function #3: (e.g., Marketing)

  - ❑ Field/Function #4:

  - ❑ Field/Function #5:

Leadership
- ❑ Listens well

- ❑ Holds respect of team and peers

- ❑ Attracts talented staff

- ❑ Articulates effectively in presentations and negotiations

- ❑ Engages team in pursuing clearly stated organizational goals

- ❑ Is biased toward action but thoughtful

NOTES & SOURCES

Foreword

1. Peter Drucker (1909–2005) was a lawyer and economist turned writer and management consultant. Widely considered to be the father of modern management, he published many books, essays, and articles. He was a popular and captivating public speaker on many topics, including economics, management, and leadership.

    Jeffrey Krames, *Inside Drucker's Brain* (Portfolio Hardcover, 2008).

Why Leadership Matters

2. John Muir (1838–1914) was a Scottish-born American naturalist. He devoted a considerable amount of his life to the preservation of United States wilderness areas. His many letters, essays, and books that vividly describe his outdoor adventures in the American West have been read widely and are still quite popular today.

    Gretel Ehrlich, *John Muir: Nature's Visionary* (National Geographic, 2000).

3. Modern Israeli history, especially from an American point of view, tends to be viewed from an obsessively pro-Israeli perspective. As I traveled throughout the Middle East as a young engineer, it was enlightening for me to encounter multiple Arab and Israeli perspectives. The passage related in this chapter was not intended to make a political statement, but it does provide a peek into another worldview. At the same time, I seek to make the point that how one leader acts can serve to inspire generations for the better. For a particularly balanced and thorough account of this region, I recommend the book *Palestine and the Arab-Israeli Conflict* written by Charles Smith

Leadership is Learned

4. Vilfredo Pareto (1848–1923) was an Italian economist and sociologist. He made important contributions as an economist in the study of income distribution and choice. He was a pacifist and an active

critic of socialist and militaristic government policy. His name is most commonly associated with the Pareto Principal, also known as the 80:20 rule.

"Vilfredo Pareto," The Library of Economics and Liberty, http://www.econlib.org/library/Enc/bios/Pareto.html (accessed 2008).

5. Henry IV (1366–1413) was King of England and France from 1399 to 1413. Shakespeare wrote two plays about Henry, whom he depicted as an embattled monarch whose claim to the throne was questioned and challenged through war, intrigue, and assassination attempts by others who wished to succeed Richard II. The bloodshed was understandable, given that Richard, who also blocked Henry from inheriting property, had exiled Henry. Henry returned from exile and conducted small wars to regain control of his lands. After amassing enough power and wealth, he declared himself rightful king and promptly deposed Richard, who died shortly after.

   William Shakespeare, *Henry IV – Part I and Part II.*

   "Henry IV of England," Wikipedia The Free Encyclopedia, http://en.wikipedia.org/wiki/Henry_IV_of_England (accessed October 26, 2008).

6. Amir Habibullah Ghazi (1890–1929) was an ethnic Tajik that briefly ruled Afghanistan after overthrowing his Pashtun predecessor. He was and continues to be considered a usurper by his detractors, including the Pashtuns, who referred to him as "son of the water carrier" because that was his father's profession. This is the equivalent to a European or American milkman at the time, which is obviously not a particularly auspicious regal lineage. Among the Tajiks, he is still remembered and respected as a legitimate ruler.

   Hafizullah Emadi, *Repression, Resistance, and Women in Afghanistan* (Praeger Publishers, 2002).

A Leadership Curriculum

7. Confucius (551–479 BCE) was a Chinese thinker and philosopher whose teachings and clever parables have influenced much of Asian social, government, and philosophical development. The focus of

his teaching was on proper behavior in families, organizations, and society in general. Some of his more pithy sayings and some that are clearly apocryphal anachronisms appear frequently in popular fortune cookies at Chinese restaurants throughout the U.S. and Europe. The actual teachings of Confucius are far more deep, rich, and insightful than those tasty little nuggets could convey.

Arthur Wailey, *The Analects of Confucius* (Vintage, 1989).

Listening

8. Epictetus (55–135) was a Stoic philosopher. Born in what is now Turkey, he was a slave in his youth, became free, and lived in Rome, and then spent much his life living and teaching in a small town in northern Greece. Some of his philosophy was recorded and published by one of his pupils, which is how we have come to know him. Epictetus taught that external events are determined by fate, but individual action is not. Therefore we are responsible for our own behavior.

    Robert Dobbin, *Epictetus: Discourses—Book 1* (Oxford University Press, USA, 2008).

9. The claimed "average" measurement of attention span varies from a few seconds to twenty minutes, depending on the source and definition of the attention span. For example, a Simon Fraser University presentation indicated that the "average continuous attention" span is thirty seconds in teens. Another researcher at the same school claimed that the "average continuous attention span of a literate human" is eight seconds. In the book, *The Exceptional Presenter*, author Timothy Koegel claims that several studies show the average "undivided attention span" is between fifteen to thirty seconds. In choosing a number as a reference, I have used the term "focused attention" defined as "rapid scanning and identification of targets" to fit with the listening exercise described in this chapter. I have chosen twenty seconds, which is in the range claimed by multiple sources and also fits my own experience in working with adults and teens.

    M. Gabier, "Computers, Education, and Children," presentation at Simon Frasier University, 2008.

Timothy J. Koegel, *The Exceptional Presenter* (Greenleaf Book Group Press, 2007).

C Mateer, M. Sohlberg, *Cognitive Rehabilitation: An Integrative Neuropsychological Approach* (The Guilford Press, 2001).

Storytelling

10. Sir Alfred Hitchcock (1899–1980) was a British filmmaker who is perhaps the most well-known and iconic filmmaker of the suspense and psychological thriller genres. Many have tried to imitate him, and few have equaled his mastery of the craft. After a long career in his native United Kingdom, he moved to Hollywood and in 1956 became an American citizen.

    "Alfred Hitchcock," MysteryNet, http://www.mysterynet.com/hitchcock/bio.shtml (accessed 2005).

11. Christopher Columbus (1451–1506) was a Genoese explorer whose voyages across the Atlantic Ocean led to a general European awareness of the American continents and the natural riches they held. He was not the first European to arrive on the American shores; Leif Ericson has received that accreditation. Despite several miserably failed attempts at establishing a settlement in the new world, Columbus initiated the process of Spanish colonization. If you visit any museum of natural history, you will almost certainly encounter a pre-Columbian exhibit, referring to the period before his arrival in the Americas.

    "Christopher Columbus," Biography, http://www.biography.com/columbus (accessed 2008).

    "Christopher Columbus," Wikipedia The Free Encyclopedia, http://en.wikipedia.org/wiki/Christopher_Columbus (accessed November 19, 2008).

12. Dr. Albert Mehrabian (1939–) conducted research at University of California, Los Angeles to determine what factors impact how people perceive our communication. His research, published in the early 1970s, showed that when we communicate feelings and emotions as a speaker, the audience perceives those feelings and emotions in three ways. Those factors have been quoted and misquoted

so often, it seems worth repeating here. Listeners perceive our emotions and feelings through words, voice, and nonverbal cues:

- ❏ 7 percent words

- ❏ 38 percent voice (tone, pace, pitch, cadence, etc.)

- ❏ 55 percent nonverbals (movement, stance, hand gestures, facial gestures, etc.)

In other words, our messages can be effectively delivered through well-chosen words but in the end, storytellers and public speakers deliver impact through what amounts to a song-and-dance routine of tone, gestures, and facial expressions. When message and impact merge, communication is truly powerful.

Timothy J. Koegel, *The Exceptional Presenter* (Greenleaf Book Group Press, 2007).

"Albert Mehrabian," Wikipedia The Free Encyclopedia, http://en.wikipedia.org/wiki/Albert_Mehrabian (accessed November 17, 2008).

13. The memory of Dr. Martin Luther King Jr. looms large, and his well-recorded actions remain a standard of greatness among leaders. His work, his mission, and above all his message of inclusiveness, which he delivered with oratory brilliance, inspired tens of millions around the world, including me. The excerpt from Dr. King's "I have a dream" speech is reprinted by arrangement with The Heirs to the Estate of Martin Luther King Jr., c/o Writers House as agent for the proprietor New York, NY. © 1963 Dr. Martin Luther King Jr.; Copyright renewed 1991 Coretta Scott King.

Negotiating

14. Gaius Cornelius Tacitus (56–120) was a senator and is considered one of the greatest historians of the Roman Empire. Like many other senators of Rome, he was a well-educated member of a wealthy, patrician family. The surviving portions of his two major works examine the state of political freedoms from the years 14 to 96 of the current era.

"Tacitus Biography," Biography, http://www.biography.com/search/article.do?id=9501109 (accessed 2008).

"Tacitus," Wikipedia The Free Encyclopedia, http://en.wikipedia. org/wiki/Tacitus (accessed November 20, 2008).

15.   Julio Olalla (1945–) is a former Chilean government lawyer and a founder of The Newfield Network, a highly respected coaching organization based in Colorado. He moved to the U.S. in 1973 to escape the Pinochet regime and began working with Fernando Flores on a theoretical and practical approach to personal transformation. The negotiation protocol language used in Chapter 6 of this book is loosely based on and somewhat different from what I learned from one of Newfield's coaches in 2000. After applying the technique for several years, I adapted some of the concepts and changed the language based on responses from my clients and business associates. In the same way, I hope readers of this book will adopt, adapt, and improve upon the outline protocol I present in this chapter.

"Founder Julio Olalla," Coach Training, Leadership Development – Newfield, http://www.newfieldnetwork.com/New/AboutNewfield/FounderJulioOlalla (accessed 2008).

"Julio Olalla," Wikipedia The Free Encyclopedia, http://en.wikipedia. org/wiki/Julio_Olalla (accessed September 24, 2007).

Assessing People

16.   Carl Gustav Jung (1875–1961) was a Swiss psychiatrist and is the founder of analytical psychology. He learned much during his time as a junior partner of Sigmund Freud. Jung emphasized understanding the psyche through exploring the worlds of dreams, art, mythology, world religion, and philosophy. Where Freud rejected religion as a fallacy and an escape, Jung came to believe that religion is a core part of our development and a vital means of communication among people. His most commonly known concepts include psychological archetypes, thanks in part to the brilliant and popular work of Joseph Campbell on the topic of mythology. Jung's other popularly known concepts are the collective unconscious and synchronicity.

"Carl (Gustav) Jung Biography," Biography, http://www.biography. com/search/article.do?id=9359134 (accessed 2008).

"Carl Jung," Wikipedia The Free Encyclopedia, http://en.wikipedia. org/wiki/Carl_jung (accessed November 1, 2008).

J. Campbell, *The Hero with a Thousand Faces* (Princeton University Press. 1973).

17. François-Marie Arouet (1694–1778), known among most people today by the pen name Voltaire, was a prolific French writer, essayist, and philosopher known for his wit, philosophical sport, and defense of civil liberties, including freedom of religion and free trade. He wrote thousands of letters and essays, was sought by monarchs for his wise and effective counsel, and was highly respected as an enlightened thinker by the educated elite throughout Europe.

"Voltaire Biography," Biography, http://www.biography.com/ search/article.do?id=9520178 (accessed 2008).

"Voltaire," Wikipedia The Free Encyclopedia, http://en.wikipedia. org/wiki/Voltaire (accessed November 22, 2008).

18. Any model on praise and criticism needs to give at least a nod to Ken Blanchard and Spencer Johnson for their seminal work on this topic. Although I am not quoting them directly, there is little doubt in my mind that my mentors were influenced by the work of these two authors, and as a result, my own training as a manager and then as a leader was indirectly influenced by their work. If you read the original blockbuster book, *The One Minute Manager,* you can see similarities with the approach I am suggesting. You will also see notable differences that come from years of practice and exposure to other approaches.

K. Blanchard and S. Johnson, *The One Minute Manager* (William Morrow, 1982).

Assembling Talent

19. Michele de Montaigne (1533–1592) was a highly respected lawyer serving in the courts of France. His essays—which in large part are self-reflecting observations about the human condition—have influenced writers, educators, and political leaders for generations. Montaigne was among the first to treat the essay as a legitimate literary genre, although at the time he was criticized for being

self indulgent. Upon retiring from his legal career in 1571, he was inducted into the prestigious order of Saint-Michel, an exclusive chivalric knighthood given by the King.

"Michel (Eyquem) de Montaigne Biography," Biography, http://www.biography.com/search/article.do?id=9412274(accessed 2008).

"Michel de Montaigne," Wikipedia The Free Encyclopedia, http://en.wikipedia.org/wiki/Montaigne (accessed November 22. 2008).

"Michel Egyuem de Montaigne," Oregon State University, http://oregonstate.edu/instruct/phl302/philosophers/montaigne.html (accessed 2008).

"Order of Saint Michael," Wikipedia The Free Encyclopedia, http://en.wikipedia.org/wiki/Order_of_Saint_Michael (accessed October 22, 2008).

20. The Hispanic gang, La eMe, also known as the Mexican Mafia, was formed in a California prison in the 1950s. The gang continues to operate despite having nearly two dozen leaders behind bars, some even in solitary confinement. La eMe is a fiercely loyal and highly disciplined organization.

Gangland, The History Channel (April-November 2008).

Will Beal, "Streat Gang Realpolitik," *The Los Angeles Times*, March 25, 2007.

"Mexican Mafia," Wikipedia The Free Encyclopedia, http://en.wikipedia.org/wiki/Mexican_Mafia (accessed December 10, 2008).

21. The battle of Agincourt was a defining moment in fifteenth-century French and English history. It was famously retold by Shakespeare in what is by far my favorite play, *Henry V.* The battle marked a turning point in weaponry and battle tactics that had been used in the Middle Ages.

William Shakespeare, *Henry V.*

"Battle of Agincourt," Wikipedia The Free Encyclopedia, http://en.wikipedia.org/wiki/Battle_of_Agincourt (accessed December 23, 2008).

22. The AIDS pandemic in Sub-Saharan Africa—which includes African counties other than Algeria, Egypt, Libya, Morocco, Tunisia, and Western Sahara—is a terrible crisis in leadership. The statistics cited primarily come from a 2007 report published by the World Health Organization. However, there are bright spots, indicating a recent improvement in creating multidisciplinary teams to tackle the problem, notably in Zimbabwe and Kenya, where the rate of HIV infection is in decline.

"AIDS Epidemic Update," *World Health Organization-UNAIDS* (December 2007).

23. For a fun yet profound read, check out Dan Pink's book *A Whole New Mind*. His main premise is that the forces of "automation, abundance, and Asia" have combined to make speed to market, efficient production, and technical prowess mere table stakes in a global marketplace. Left brain prowess is not enough; you also need to sharpen your right brain. If you doubt this, witness the ridiculous success of the beautifully designed yet expensive iPod and iPhone from Apple. Fortunately, he gives us more than theory; he tells stories, provides exercises, and suggests additional reading.

Dan Pink, *A Whole New Mind* (Riverhead Hardcover, 2005).

Reaching Agreement

24. Robert H. Estabrook (1918–) is an American journalist, author, and editor. He is perhaps best remembered for his service as chief foreign correspondent for the *Washington Post* during the early 1960s, when the U.S. repeatedly battled with the USSR in the media, in the world of espionage, and in diplomatic circles. Estabrook's substantial articles and opinions figure prominently in the JFK Library archives.

"Robert Estabrook," *Reference Volume: Contemporary Authors— Biography* (Thomas Gale, January 1, 2004).

Nicholas Daniloff, *Of Spies and Spokesman* (University of Missouri Press, 2008).

25. During a Myers-Briggs workshop, the facilitator told me that most CEOs are introverts. Since then I have been told similar nuggets of introvert-to-CEO correlation by consultants specializing in DiSC, Enneagram, and 5Dynamics. Apparently there is at least some truth to this anecdotal insight; *USA Today* published an article that claimed studies showed that about half of all CEOs were introverts. My own experience would say that is an understatement—few leaders I have met are extroverts. In any case, I chose to go with the more conservative estimate from *USA Today* because that is the only legitimate source I could find.

    Dell Jones, "Not all Successful CEOs are Extroverts," *USA Today* (June 7, 2007).

26. *The American Heritage Dictionary* defines introvert as "a person whose thoughts and interests are directed inward," but introversion is not the same as shyness. Introverts prefer solitary activities, in particular when it comes to regeneration and recuperation, whereas shy people avoid social encounters due to anxiety.

    Meredith Whitten, "All About Shyness," *Psychology Central* (August 21, 2001).

27. Scott McNealy (1954–) is still the Chairman of Sun Microsystems, a computer and technology company he co-founded in 1982 together with Vinod Khosla, Bill Joy, and Andy Bechtolsheim. Sun was one of many successful companies launched in Silicon Valley during the 1980s and contributed significantly to the formation of the current technology landscape. As a sales representative for Oracle in the early 1990s, I felt privileged and proud to be a partner with the well-run and innovative Sun Microsystems.

Making Tough Choices

28. Socrates (c. 469–399 BCE) was a classical Greek philosopher and is often hailed as one of the founders of Western philosophy. He lived during a time of oral teaching, so committed none of his own thoughts to paper. As a result, he is known primarily through the stories written by his student Plato. It is this idealized Socrates,

immortalized by Plato, that we give credit to for the concepts of Socratic irony and the Socratic Method itself. Every dialogue written by Plato is worth reading, but in particular I found that *Phaedo* was the most moving. In *Phaedo*, Plato painted a brave and wise picture of Socrates as he faced a certain and unjust death sentence.

The Portable Plato, ed. S. Buchannan (Penguin, 1977).

29. The story of Scott Paper, which faced declining margins in an ever more commoditized market, took the bold risk to transform itself from a paper supplier largely serving the printing industry into a high margin consumer goods company. This transformation is well described in Jim Collins' book, *Built to Last.*

J. Collins and J. Porras, *Built to Last: Successful Habits of Visionary Companies* (Harper Business, 1994).

30. The story in this book about Julius Caesar at the Rubicon is admittedly my own fanciful retelling of this famous event. The definitive account was written by Suetonius, the Roman historian, and has been retold countless times in many historical accounts and historical fictions. I have stayed true to the main facts, but have embellished with some bits of descriptive detail that seem plausible, at least to me.

"Julius Caesar," Wikipedia The Free Encyclopedia, http://en.wikipedia.org/wiki/Julius_Caesar (accessed December 8, 2008).

"Legio XIII Gemina," Wikipedia The Free Encyclopedia, http://en.wikipedia.org/wiki/Legio_XIII_Gemina (accessed December 8, 2008).

"Rubicon," Wikipedia The Free Encyclopedia, http://en.wikipedia.org/wiki/Rubicon (accessed December 8, 2008).

Harnessing Ambition

31. Lao Tzu (500BCE?) was a philosopher of ancient China and is a central figure in Taoism. The *Tao Te Ching*, allegedly written or assembled by Lao Tzu, is a text filled with deep wisdom and is one of a small group of texts that serve as the central teachings of Taoism. When Buddhist monks arrived in China, they found a receptive

audience among the Taoists. The two religious and philosophical traditions merged and became Ch'an Buddhism, which was then brought to Korea as *Soen* and also to Japan as *Zen*.

Gia-fe Feng and J. English, *Tao Te Ching* (Vintage Book, 1972).

Zen Master Seung Sahn, *The Compass of Zen* (Shambhala, 1997).

P. Merel, "7. Complete," *TaoDeChing-Lao Tze.*, http://www.chinapage.com/gnl.html (accessed 2008)

32. J. Bick, "Microsoft Millionaires Come of Age," *New York TImes*, May 29, 2005.

33. Kenneth Lay (1942–2006) was a veteran executive of the energy industry, infamously known as the CEO and chairman of Enron. He led both the meteoric rise and sudden downfall of that company. The name Enron became synonymous with the accounting fraud perpetrated by the company and also led to the dissolution of Arthur Anderson, one of the most prestigious accounting firms in the world. Although he was convicted on several counts of fraud, Lay died of heart failure before his sentencing.

   "Kenneth L. Lay, Ex-Chairman of Enron, Dies," *New York Times*, July 5, 2006.

34. Bishop Desmond Tutu (1931–) was ordained as an Anglican priest in 1960. In 1975 he was appointed Dean of St. Mary's Cathedral in Johannesburg, the first black to hold that position. From 1976 to 1978, he was Bishop of Lesotho and in 1985 became the first black archbishop making him the leader of South Africa's entire Anglican congregation. Bishop Tutu has lived by a publically declared mission to promote "a democratic and just society without racial divisions." He was awarded the Nobel Prize in 1984 and the Gandhi Peace Price in 2005.

   "Desmond Tutu Biography," Nobel Prize Foundation, http://nobelprize.org/nobel_prizes/peace/laureates/1984/tutu-bio.html.

   "Desmond Tutu," Wikipedia The Free Encyclopedia, http://en.wikipedia.org/wiki/Desmond_Tutu (accessed January 29, 2009).

"Desmond (Mpilo) Tutu Biography," Biography, http://www.biography.com/search/article.do?id=9512516 (accessed 2009).

35. Jim Bakker (1940–) is a pastor and televangelist once highly regarded by other leaders of the evangelical Christian community and by his congregation. He and his wife Tammy Faye were seen by millions on weekly television programs, including *Praise The Lord* and *The 700 Club*, the latter of which still airs today but is now led by other evangelical ministers. Bakker was convicted of several counts of fraud, sentenced, served time, and is now remarried and working once again as a televangelist, with a much smaller following.

"Jim Bakker," Wikipedia The Free Encyclopedia, http://en.wikipedia.org/wiki/Jim_Bakker (accessed October 22, 2008).

36. Adolf Hitler (1889–1945) is by no means the only leader who ever abused his power, perpetrated genocide, conducted horrific war, or preached the superiority of his nation. But he is without doubt the best known and most often used icon for self-centered, deluded leadership.

"Adolf Hitler Biography," Biography, http://www.biography.com/search/article.do?id=9340144 (accessed 2008).

37. Mahatma Ghandi (1869–1948) was the primary political leader in India as it fought for independence and was also revered as a spiritual force. His focus on mass civil disobedience, based on a vow of non-violence, inspired many civil-rights and freedom movements around the world. He is a superb example of leadership in action.

Richard Attenborough, *Gandhi* (1982) film.

"Mahatma (Mohandas Karamchand) Gandhi Biography," Biography, http://www.biography.com/search/article.do?id=9305898 (accessed 2008).

Appendix A – Hiring a Coach

38. According to Ken Blanchard, "Seagull Managers fly in, make a lot of noise, dump on everyone, and then fly out." There were a number of variations on this expression, popular before he put it in his book. For example, I heard a similar phrase applied to consultants

many years ago, along the lines of "Consultants are like ducks. They fly in, poop over everything, and fly out." Coaches are not as noisy as seagulls or skittish as ducks, so I used the more apt pigeons in yet another variation on this bird metaphor.

K. Blanchard, *Leadership and the One Minute Manager* (Harper-Collins Business, 1999).

39. Here are three examples of studies that quantify the economic benefit from coaching:

❑   In a 1997 study of thirty-one managers who received conventional management training, those who received training alone increased productivity by 22 percent whereas mangers who received coaching combined with training increased productivity by 88 percent, indicating a four-fold improvement from coaching.

G. Olivero, "Executive coaching as a transfer of training tool: Effects on productivity in a public agency," *International Personnel Management Association* (1997)

❑   In a 2001 study of a hundred executives who had received coaching, the ROI was over 500 percent with tangible gains in productivity and quality validated by peers and stakeholders.

J. McGovern et al., "Maximizing the impact of executive coaching: Behavioral change, organizational outcomes and return on investment," *Manchester Review* (2001).

❑   In a recent multi-year study of executives in a U.S.-based company, the average ROI of an executive coaching program ranged between 600 percent and 1000 percent, with an experienced coach and explicit goal setting.

Dembkowski, Eldridge, and Hunter, *The Seven Steps of Effective Executive Coaching* (Thorogood, 2006).

About the Author

Michael Schutzler is a successful business coach with more than a dozen years experience coaching and mentoring CEOs, executives, and board members.

Michael developed a passion for and expertise in leadership over the course of twenty-five years in a wide variety of executive and management roles in notable companies, including Harris Corporation, RR Donnelley & Sons, Classmates.com, and RealNetworks. He has travelled extensively throughout Asia, the Middle-East, and Europe. As an independent venture investor, he has helped launch more than a dozen Internet and technology companies. Michael has also served in leadership roles in nonprofit organizations and public school committees. He holds an MBA in Finance and Economics from the W. E. Simon School at University of Rochester and a BS in Electrical Engineering from Pennsylvania State University.

Learn more about Michael's professional background and business coaching practice at www.BlueSevenPartners.com

You can follow Michael on twitter @schutzler